DÜRER

Martin Schön Conterfeit

SPRING ART BOOKS

DÜRER

BY ALLAN BRAHAM

SPRING BOOKS · LONDON

ACKNOWLEDGMENTS

The works in this volume are reproduced by kind permission of the following collections and galleries to which they belong: Albertina, Vienna (Figures 1, 12, 13; Plates 6, 7, 9, 12, 29, 32); The Ashmolean Museum, Oxford (Plate 5); Bayerische Staatsbibliothek, Munich (Plate 42); Bayerische Staatsgemäldesammlungen, Munich (Plates 15, 16, 21, 23, 50); Fondazione Giorgio Cini, Venice (Figure 15); Gallerie Pontificie, Vatican City (Figure 16); Gemäldegalerie, Kassel (Plate 22); Germanisches Nationalmuseum, Nuremberg (Plates 14, 40); Graphische Sammlung der Universitätsbibliothek, Erlangen (Frontispiece); Historisches Museum, Frankfurt (Plate 35); Kunsthistorisches Museum, Vienna (Plates 24, 34, 36, 38, 41, 45); Louvre, Paris (Plates 3, 4); Louvre, Cabinet des Dessins (Plate 48); Musée Bonnat, Bayonne (Figure 14); Musée Condé, Chantilly (Figure 9; Plates 37, 47); National Gallery, Prague (Plates 27, 28); National Gallery of Art, Washington, Samuel H. Kress Collection (Plates 18, 19); Prado, Madrid (Plates 20, 33, 43); Staatliche Kunstsammlungen, Dresden (Plate 13); Stiftung Preussischer Kulturbesitz, Staatliche Museen, Kupferstichkabinett, Berlin-Dahlem (Plates 2, 8, 30); Stiftung Preussischer Kulturbesitz, Staatliche Museen, Gemäldegalerie, Berlin-Dahlem (Plates 25, 26, 39, 44); Thyssen Collection, Lugano (Plate 31); The Trustees of the British Museum, London (Figures 2, 3, 4, 5, 6, 7, 8, 10, 11; Plates 10, 11, 46); Uffizi, Florence (Plates 1, 17, 49). The following photographs were supplied by Photo Aubert, Bayonne (Figure 14); Joachim Blauel, Munich (Plates 15, 16, 21, 23, 50); Fritz Brieke, Frankfurt-am-Main (Plate 35); Cine Brunel, Lugano (Plate 31); Photographie Giraudon, Paris (Figure 9; Plate 37); Michael Holford, London (Plates 10, 11, 46); Jacqueline Hyde, Paris (Plates 3, 4, 47, 48); Erwin Meyer, Vienna (Plates 24, 34, 36, 38, 41, 45); Ladislav Neubert, Prague (Plates 27, 28); Scala, Florence (Plates 1, 17, 40, 49); Walter Steinkopf, Berlin (Plates 2, 8, 30, 39).

First Published 1965
2nd Impression 1966

Published by

SPRING BOOKS

Drury House · Russell Street · London WC 2

© Paul Hamlyn Ltd. 1965

Printed in Czechoslovakia by Polygrafia, Prague

T 1722

Contents

Black and White Illustrations

Introduction

Dürer is an artist who rewards close study. His works are not only superbly competent and often of great charm but they are in addition a never-ending source of fascination to the interpreter. Every aspect of his character and intelligence is clearly expressed in a tremendously varied and copious output. As a German artist and an instinctive draughtsman, Dürer developed the northern skills of woodcutting and engraving to unparalleled heights, he undertook fearlessly to learn from the achievements of the Italian Renaissance, developed an unusual interest in the experiments of Venetian painters into effects of colour and light and came to terms with the ideals of the High Renaissance. His works also reflect the gradual emergence of Dürer as a humanist scholar while at the same time expressing the intensity of his religious convictions and revealing many of his personal characteristics, as they are shown in his writings; his vanity, a love of curiosities of all descriptions and occasional outbursts of fantasy.

Dürer's career can be considered in seven parts: four long periods of work in his native town of Nuremberg and three shorter periods spent abroad. This division corresponds with profound changes of outlook, for travel brought Dürer new interests and ambitions which can be seen transforming the character of his work.

Albrecht Dürer was born in Nuremberg on 21st May, 1471, the third son of Albrecht Dürer, a goldsmith of Hungarian origin, who had settled in Nuremberg in 1455 and had there, twelve years later, married Barbara Holper the daughter of the master for whom he was working. The boy began his training in his father's workshop, but in 1486 he became an apprentice to Michael Wolgemut, the most important local painter (plate 40). Dürer stayed with Wolgemut until early in 1490 when he left Nuremberg on a "bachelor journey" to gain experience working with other artists elsewhere.

The earliest surviving record of Dürer's talent during this period is the famous *Self Portrait* drawn at the age of 13 in 1484 (figure 1 on page 9). Although timid and over-wrought, the drawing shows Dürer's unusually precocious ability as a draughtsman, an ability not only to represent faithfully a given image but also to render it with an instinctive sense of design, which is not found in similar drawings attributed to his father. Clearly Dürer must have felt that the trade of a painter would better suit his interests and considerable talents than that of a goldsmith. This drawing also foreshadows two characteristics of the artist, both unusual at the time and both to become more pronounced; the production of drawings not merely for working purposes but as a visual record of the artist's experience and, connected with this, Dürer's unusually great interest in himself.

Dürer must have realised later that his training had been inadequate in many ways and later on in his life he proposed, but never finished, a comprehensive treatise on painting for the benefit of the young artist, in which he intended to explain skills which he had learnt at great effort long after his own apprenticeship. The idea itself of such a treatise, based as it was on Italian and classical writings (but with a fair mixture of astrology and common sense) was quite alien to the workshop tradition in which Dürer had been brought up and it implied much that would have been revolutionary. The painter should have a general education and learn Latin, for example, and he should make a thorough study of proportion and perspective. Disciplines like these, but self-taught, were to play an important part in Dürer's life, giving him a greater control over his work and raising him from the status of a tradesman to that of a scholar.

Plates 1 and 2 show two aspects of Dürer's art in the last year of this apprenticeship. The portrait of his father (1490) has something of the hesitant and charming quality of the early self-portrait of 1484. The sitter is shown in prayer looking fixedly to the left and with a rosary in his hands, but both gesture and expression are cramped and the figure has little solidity.The head and hands resemble elaborate drawings carefully attached to the unfilled clothes. The landscape drawing (plate 2) of *The Wire-Drawing Mill* near Nuremberg is more exceptional. Studies like these, of actual places, must have been very rare, if they were attempted at all, and the existence of several examples by Dürer at this time shows an unusual singlemindedness and a spontaneous enthusiasm for the subject which were to be richly rewarded in the next few years. The relative lack of composition in the present drawing has suggested connections with the landscape backgrounds in earlier Nuremberg pictures and Dürer's principal aim was probably for topographical accuracy. The buildings and trees are carefully outlined in pen and ink but the flat surfaces are more freely indicated with water-colour, resulting in a certain tension between this more generalised and evocative medium and the precise pen lines.

Dürer returned to Nuremberg for only a few months in the five years between 1490 and 1495. It was therefore his longest and perhaps most significant period of travel. Where the young artist spent the first year and a half is not known but he may have gone to the Rhine area and to Holland. In 1492 he arrived in Colmar, in search of Martin Schongauer, then the most important German painter and engraver but only to find that he had just died. He then proceeded to Basle, the main centre of publishing in Europe, where he stayed with Georg Schongauer, one of the brothers of Martin. In 1493 he left for Strasbourg whence he returned home in the following year and was married to Agnes Frey. His visit home was short, however, and he set off for Venice in the same year, returning home finally in 1495.

Comparatively few works have survived from this period but they show a mar
change of outlook. He was employed in Basle to make woodcut illustrations for book
a process which would have been made familiar to him in Nuremberg by Wolgemut
by Dürer's own godfather, Anton Koberger, the foremost publisher in Germany.
journey to Venice, an unusual pilgrimage for a young Northern artist at that time, must have been inspired by a growing interest in the achievements of Italian art which increased in scope as Dürer began, in Venice, to copy the more violent works of Italian artists like Mantegna and to absorb the ideas of the Renaissance, including ideals of

8

1. *Self Portrait*

2. *St John before God and the Elders*

3. *Adam and Eve*

4. *Assumption and Coronation of the Virgin*

5. *Christ presented to the People*
(from "The Small Passion")

6. *Christ presented to the People*
(from "The Engraved Passion")

7. *St Jerome in his Study*

8. *"Melancolia. I."*

9. *The Imperial Herald, Caspar Sturm; Landscape with a Castle*

10. *Agony in the Garden*

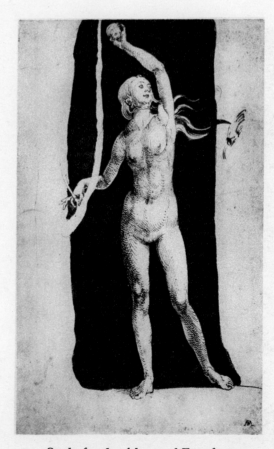

11. *Knight, Death and Devil*

12. *Study for the Adam and Eve of 1507*

13. *Adoration of the Kings*

14. *Madonna with Eight Saints*

15. Giovanni Bellini:
The San Zaccaria Altarpiece

16. Raphael: *The Coronation of the Virgin*

beauty rediscovered from antiquity and probably methods of artificial perspective also.

The second of Dürer's self-portraits dates from the beginning of his travels (frontispiece). Drawn hastily on the back of a sheet with a study of the Holy Family, it shows the artist in a mood of despondency, which it is tempting to interpret as the result of a personal or artistic conflict, but which reveals at least a more intense self-awareness than the earliest self-portrait drawing, and a greater interest in psychological expressiveness set down with an eye for the essential and revealing detail. The first painted *Self Portrait* (plate 3) is of 1493; executed originally on vellum, it was probably intended as a wedding portrait to be sent home to Dürer's future wife, for the artist holds a sprig of Eryngium, symbolising love. He portrays himself in an elaborate jacket and undershirt, intended perhaps to convey a new status. Dürer was always extremely conscious of his own dress, and it is described in great detail in this portrait. Even so there is a grasp of anatomy, of a physical object inhabiting space, more apparent here than in the portrait of Dürer's father of three years before.

Perhaps the most highly prized works of this period are Dürer's landscape studies in water-colour. Many were executed during the journeys to and from Venice (plate 4); they differ in character considerably from the earlier landscapes. The views are chosen with more care for the design of the finished drawing, and wash, laid on in richer colours, predominates over the pen lines, thus conveying the atmospheric properties of the scene more effectively. Some of the drawings (plate 5) are finished in haste and, freed from the tyranny of topographical accuracy, Dürer uses broad areas of water-colour, laid on with astonishing freedom, to complete the scenes.

Once returned to Nuremberg, Dürer embarked on the production of a vast number of works in all media, many of which made his name famous throughout Europe. He acquired a workshop with apprentices to help with the more laborious work, and became a master, receiving commissions from fellow citizens and German princes.

Water-colours, however, were not neglected and they dwindle in number only after about 1503. Many of them provided material which was used later in engravings and other projects and Dürer seems to have kept them as a source of ideas for landscapes, figures and animals drawn directly from nature. The *Soldier on Horseback* (plate 6), drawn in 1498 as an unerring description of the colours and forms of an everyday sight, reappears in an engraving of 1513 (figure 11 on page 11), transformed into movement and in a complex symbolical disguise. Other figure drawings in water-colour are records of the clothes worn by contemporaries, like the ravishing study (plate 7) of a *Nuremberg Woman dressed for Church*.

The drawings contained also a record of curiosities and strange animals, a neverending source of pleasure to Dürer. The *Lobster* (plate 8) of 1495 was perhaps drawn in Venice. It seems to advance across the page with open pincers and an expression of heightened malice. More restrained is the *Young Hare* (plate 9), a famous drawing of 1502, which is observed in such breathtaking detail, even taking in the reflections of a window in the protruding eyes of the animal. Landscape drawings continued to occupy Dürer's attention after his return to Nuremberg, but he now saw his native town with all the atmospheric richness of the Italian Alps. The "Weier Haus" (plate 10) is one of the most famous studies of this period and this is, perhaps, because while it has the spontaneity of the other drawings it is also more elaborately composed and finished (almost like a painting by Ruisdael). The sky is filled in as fully as the land and only the foreground, which seems always to have created a problem for the artist, remains unpainted. *The Pond in the Woods* of 1495/6 (plate 11) is equally exceptional. Although probably suggested by an actual place, the drawing seems principally to be a study of the drama of nature and in this respect is far in advance of its date.

Dürer rarely used water-colour as a medium for studies of composition but the great exception here is the drawing of about 1503 (plate 12) of *The Virgin with a Multitude of Animals*. It may be, however, that colour was essential to the meaning of the picture, for the striking element is the comprehensiveness of the scene. Not only animals, but plants too are shown in great variety and the landscape comprises almost every geographical component. The sky also is unusually full of clouds of all descriptions encircling a star in the centre. The Nativity theme with the Annunciation to the shepherds in the background seems to be combined therefore with a thanksgiving for the birth of Christ in which the whole of nature takes part.

In more serious activities, Dürer's greatest achievement during his first years as a master in Nuremberg was probably in the field of woodcutting. Apart from single sheets, he produced or began three series of woodcut illustrations. The earliest of these was the *Apocalypse* (figure 2 on page 9), a sequence of 15 illustrations, apparently all cut by Dürer himself and printed and bound at his own instigation in book form, with the corresponding text on the back of each plate. In these pictures, Dürer seems to have brought to life the unconvincing figures of earlier prints. His scenes are often of enormous complexity but organised with an unerring eye for the dramatic glance and gesture and combined in many cases with vignettes of landscape as detailed and evocative as many of the Alpine water-colours.

No less astonishing is Dürer's achievement in engraving in these years. Engraving had been made famous as a medium by Schongauer and this was probably one of the reasons why Dürer had been drawn to Colmar in 1492. It was a more flexible medium than woodcutting, and capable of more precise and sophisticated effects than even painting. More expensive to buy than woodcuts, the engravings appealed to a more educated audience and were generally chosen by Dürer to give to admirers. Thus Dürer reserved engravings for his more intellectual statements; in later years they contain many of his recondite and obscure themes while in this first Nuremberg period a large number show the results of experiments inspired by what he had learnt in Italy and from contacts with Italian artists in the north. There are engravings devoted not only to scenes of classical mythology but those in which perspective or the study of the human figure or that of the horse is the main subject. Perhaps the most famous such plate is the *Adam and Eve* of 1504 (figure 3 on page 9) where the male figure, for example, derives from studies by Dürer based on the Apollo Belvedere. The Latin inscription on this plate reads like a challenge by an artist proud to describe himself as German ("Noricus" — from the name of the Roman province of Noricum, approximating to Bavaria south of the Danube), who has recreated in the medium associated with northern artists like Schongauer, and in a Christian context, the heroic figures of classical antiquity. With Dürer, as with other northern artists (Rubens, for example), such ability to compete with Italians on their own ground was achieved only after years of intense study and even then an irrepressible vitality is never absent, even from their actual copies. So, here, the figures frown in concentration and stand in a dense northern forest, which crawls

14

with various animals probably included as an allegory of the four temperaments which mankind had inherited from its first parents.

In painting, Dürer was much less of an innovator. The earliest known religious work is the *Dresden Altarpiece* (plate 13) of 1496, painted for Dürer's principal patron at this time, Frederick the Wise of Saxony. The figure group is probably Italian in inspiration but it is set in an interior that is distinctly Flemish in appearance. The viewpoint is an unusually high one and consequently there is little overlapping in the figures, who appear isolated and spread across the surface of the picture. Dürer has used pale size colours instead of oil paint and they leave the grain of the canvas showing and thus emphasise the flatness of the picture surface. The architecture plays the chief role in the articulation of the picture and it is organised as an artificial perspective construction which is not wholly convincing at floor level. *The Paumgärtner Altarpiece* of about 1502/4 (plate 15) is of a similar subject showing the Nativity of Christ in the central panel and again the architecture predominates over the figures, forming a long corridor of space into the picture. The figures, however, are fitted carefully into the architectural scheme and form a clearly defined pyramid in the foreground, but each is seen in isolation and gives the effect of an almost joyful instability. They are framed by the rows of portraits of the donors and their children, while the wings (plate 16) may show other members of the family dressed as St George and St Eustace. The wings are often believed to have been painted slightly before the centre panel but they have some of the grandeur lacking in the latter, the saints standing in carefully contrasting attitudes like guards protecting the central scene and looking down into it with watchful respect.

In Dürer's third early painting of the Nativity theme, *The Adoration of the Kings* of 1504 (plate 17), the viewpoint is lower and the picture is organised in terms of the figures themselves, who are more securely posed and form a stable group of interlocking pyramid shapes in the foreground. The welter of descriptive detail and the psychological effusion of the scene are actually intensified but the figure group predominates and only after carefully examining the picture does one take in the brace securing the last stone of the broken arch or the elaborate cups carried by two of the kings, the braying donkey or Christ's impatient gesture to open the box offered by the kneeling king. The main figure group dominates in colour also; Dürer was opposed in theory, but not always in practice, to refinements of colour, preferring to use a few colours in their full intensity and here the reds, blues, and greens of the draperies in the foreground stand out against the neutral grey and brown tones of the background. Compared with *The Paumgärtner Altarpiece* (plate 15), it is clear that Dürer's style has undergone a remarkable change and there can be little doubt that the influence of Leonardo da Vinci (1452-1519) played some part in this transformation. Some of the elements in the present picture are strikingly Leonardesque in character while others, the figure of the kneeling king in particular, resemble motifs in Leonardo's unfinished *Adoration of the Kings* of about 1480. Not only did Dürer know a great deal about Leonardo's work but there are also some striking parallels between the two men. Both were intensely interested in the cultivation of their own minds and personalities; both made drawings as records of their personal experiences and amongst the earliest works of each are studies of landscape. One tends therefore to link them not only as artists, but also as phenomena of the times in which they lived.

The *Hercules killing the Stymphalian Birds* of about 1500 (plate 14), which like the Dresden altarpiece, is painted in size colours, confirms the impression of the course of Dürer's development given by his Nativity pictures. The painting may conceivably have been one of a series made to decorate a room for Frederick the Wise. There was, however, little demand in Germany for large scale mythological pictures, although smaller scenes were produced in large numbers with frankly erotic intentions by Lucas Cranach.

Only one other example by Dürer is known, the *Lucretia* at Munich, completed in 1518. The present picture is close in style to Antonio Pollaiuolo (c. 1432-1498), a Florentine painter well known for his skill as a draughtsman of energetic nudes conceived almost entirely in terms of outline, with little internal modelling. Dürer was familiar with Pollaiuolo's work from engravings and, faced with the subject of Hercules, must have thought instinctively of the Florentine artist. The effect in this picture — the main subject spreading like a silhouette against a landscape panorama, which is characteristic of Dürer's early pictures — was reinforced in this case by the influence of Pollaiuolo. The result may have seemed more intelligible as part of a decorative ensemble.

Dürer achieved a greater degree of competence at an earlier stage in smaller religious works and portraits than in his narrative pictures. The *Madonna and Child* of about 1498 (plate 19) appears to be the only small picture of this subject painted by Dürer in this period and it cannot have been executed long after his return from Venice, being, of all Dürer's small Madonnas, the most Italian in the disposition of the figures. It may even have been directly inspired by a particular model, though Venetian groups in which the Virgin actually carries her son are rare. The richness of the setting, the marble and elaborate mouldings would in an Italian picture decorate the frame of a throne, but Dürer turns these improbable elements into a room as convincing, at first sight, as many an interior in Netherlandish pictures. Furthermore, despite the Italian influence in the poses of the figures, they are drawn with all Dürer's incisive precision and, in parts like the silhouette of the child or the cushion beneath his feet, the forms swell with a barely concealed energy. On the reverse of the panel (plate 18) is a representation of *Lot and his Daughters fleeing from Sodom*, perhaps painted earlier than the Madonna. Dürer has thought with his usual care to provide the fugitives with all that they might need for their journey and more besides. Except for the turban worn by Lot, the figures could have been derived almost verbatim from studies made of his fellow citizens (plate 7). The landscape, however, is not close to Dürer's water-colour studies, being built up elaborately in sections to cover the whole surface of the picture, and showing in one compartment the thoroughgoing destruction of the two cities of the plain.

According to Dürer, the duties of painting were shared between religious art and portraiture. A large number of portraits survive from all stages of his career and although he excelled as a portraitist, Dürer was no great innovator, restricting his interest almost entirely to the person of the sitter. He seems to have felt little urge to experiment, like his near-contemporary Holbein for example, with new types of portrait. This is not to say that Dürer's productions are at all monotonous, for they reflect changes in his style, often with unusual clarity. The *Self Portrait* (plate 20) of 1498 shows the artist in a setting similar to that of the *Madonna and Child* (plate 19), and this adds an element of grandeur to what is basically the same figure as in the *Self Portrait* (plate 3) of 1493, although the clothes are now smarter and the hair is arranged in elaborate and presumably artificial curls. Dürer also wears gloves, which must be an almost unique feature in a self-portrait and suggests that it is a record of the painter looking at his very best.

16

The picture is constructed with unusual care. The curve of an arch frames the back of the head and the cord of Dürer's cloak, carefully twisted near his shoulder, runs along the fringe of the hair, parallel with the line of the arm at the base. The light comes not from the window but from inside the room and it throws a shadow irrationally across the window-ledge from inside. In its complicated construction this portrait differs considerably from Dürer's next *Self Portrait* of 1500 (plate 21) which is more direct, though seemingly close to it in mood. Here Dürer faces the spectator in full-face, an attitude generally reserved for hieratic pictures of Christ as "Salvator Mundi" and it has been thought that Dürer intended this picture to convey the meaning, which is to be met with in Italian writings on art, that the artist can be likened to God since both are creators. Hence, perhaps, the emphasis in this portrait on Dürer's right hand and index finger.

In other portraits of this time, Dürer adopts a third convention in which the sitter appears before a cloth of honour and against a landscape background. The *Portrait of Elspeth Tucher* (plate 21) is a straightforward essay in this setting, although Dürer turns the pattern of the brocade background round the back of the head, a falsification of nature made in the interests of the design. In the contemporary *Portrait of Oswolt Krell* of 1499 (plate 23) the backdrop is a plain bright red in colour and there is no parapet dividing the sitter from the landscape, which now has high trees in the foreground whose rich foliage fills up the surface of the picture, almost as a compensation for the simplicity of the cloth background. The portrait forms the centre of the triptych, an unusual but not unprecedented arrangement, and the wings show the arms of the sitter supported by monstrous hairy wild men brandishing clubs who are, perhaps, incarnations of the charge on the right hand shield.

Dürer had already assimilated much that Italy had to teach him when in 1505 he again visited Venice and stayed for almost two years. He was now a famous artist, known and appreciated abroad for his woodcuts and engravings. In Venice he made contacts with the chief painters of the city, Giovanni Bellini amongst them, as Dürer relates in a series of letters sent to Nuremberg to his close friend Willibald Pirkheimer. Dürer was still in search of knowledge from Italian theorists and his writings on art begin shortly after his return to Nuremberg. At the same time, however, he was better equipped to appreciate the achievements of contemporary Venetian painting. Since his last visit to Venice, a new generation of painters, headed by the old Giovanni Bellini, had begun to introduce an altogether softer and more monumental style, and their influence on Dürer, especially on his use of colour, is perhaps rather unexpectedly strong.

In two famous female portraits executed in all probability in Venice (plates 24 and 25), the sitters have a modesty and reflectiveness not apparent until now in Dürer's portraits. The second picture, with the initials A.D. sewn on the bodice, is treated with a softness that complements Dürer's interpretation of the character of the sitter. The paint gives the impression of having been stippled over the surface of the face to evoke the texture of flesh. The atmosphere of the picture is extraordinarily Venetian, with an almost abstract background of sea and sky, but it is more than a mere background to the picture, for Dürer clearly suggests by his handling of the light that the sitter is actually in the open air. This effect is achieved by the unusual variety in the densities of the lights and shadows, giving the effect of light playing all around the form of the head and also stressing its solidity. There are, furthermore, areas where Dürer shows strong reflected lights, as on the necklace in the shadow of the head, while the lace shoulder-bands are painted with great freedom to suggest a stronger light breaking up their formal pattern. On the other hand, the actual contours of the forms are scarcely softened at all but drawn with Dürer's customary sharpness. It should be admitted that this picture is somewhat worn but even so it cannot originally have lacked all its present virtuosity, for other works of this time also show how strongly Dürer had responded to the experiments of Venetian painters like Giovanni Bellini and Giorgione into effects of colour and light.

The *Virgin with the Siskin* (plate 26) of 1506 probably derives from an Italian picture, but the theme of St John handing lilies of the valley to the Christ Child is actually interpreted with all Dürer's characteristic effusion. The colours, however, are softer and more varied and this is especially noticeable in the landscape. The tree on the right, for example, if compared with those in the *Portrait of Oswolt Krell* (plate 23) of three years earlier, partakes more of the character of a water-colour, with few contour lines in the foliage and an altogether freer application of paint.

The most important of Dürer's Venetian pictures was the *Feast of the Rose-Garlands* (Rosenkranzfest), painted in 1506 for the high altar of S. Bartolomeo, the church of the German colony in Venice and existing today in a much repainted condition in the Prague National Gallery (plate 27). The subject is an unusual one showing the Virgin and Child enthroned and distributing garlands of roses to the kneeling figures of the Pope, Julius II, and the Holy Roman emperor and German king, Maximilian I, in the foreground, while a gathering composed of members of the German community in Venice receive garlands from cherubim and St Dominic, who was personally associated with the devotion of the rosary. In the background on the right stands the figure of the artist, present presumably as a member of the German community. He takes no part in the action but carries a paper inscribed with his name in Latin and a claim that the work had been painted in five months. Dürer's letters show how pleased he was with the altarpiece, with the pace at which it had been carried out and with the colouring which he had deliberately applied in the Venetian manner.

The picture is indeed remarkable, being much more than a merely successful attempt by a northerner at painting an Italian altarpiece. Dürer has combined in the design two of the most formal types of Venetian altarpiece, the votive picture where a kneeling figure is introduced to the Virgin and Child and the "sacra conversazione" where the Virgin and Child sit enthroned in the centre (often with angels at their feet) and surrounded by the standing figures of saints. Dürer's picture is thus a votive picture conceived in terms of a "sacra conversazione" with kneeling figures disposed symmetrically around the Virgin and Child. In addition, the subject gave scope to Dürer's ability to express physical action convincingly and to his talents as a portraitist and landscape painter. He has conceived the action taking place entirely in a landscape setting and it is in this respect that the picture differs most radically from the Venetian altarpiece tradition. He uses tree trunks cut off beneath the leaves (plate 28) where an Italian would use columns and they frame the canopy of the Virgin's throne which again is not an architectural feature but made of cloth and held up in the air by cherubim, and more convincing therefore as an improvisation in a landscape setting. The colours of the picture are apparently unusually luminous and make it easier to believe that the scene is taking place in the open with the figures grouped on the grass beneath the trees. For the mantle of the pope, Dürer made a preliminary study in water-colour (plate 29) and the use of such a medium shows how the artist was thinking more in terms of colour than of line. The other surviving studies are black and white brush drawings, like the one for the figure of the architect on the left of the composition (plate 30). This was the more usual medium for Dürer's preparatory drawings, but they are sketched on a particular blue Venetian paper which is evocative of the landscape atmosphere of the finished picture.

It is a measure of Dürer's achievement that the *Rosenkranzfest* must be considered in relation to the development of Italian painting, not merely as a derivative work, but as a Renaissance picture in its own right. For in the conception and disposition of its figures, the picture is close in spirit to contemporary Italian works like Bellini's *San Zaccaria Altarpiece* (figure 15 on page 12) where the new harmony and amplitude of the High Renaissance is already apparent. Dürer was the first and almost the only northern artist to approach at all closely this fulfilment of the Renaissance style, and, when given a suitable theme in his later German altarpieces, he continued to develop its principles.

The third of Dürer's Venetian religious pictures, the *Christ among the Doctors* of 1506 (plate 31) is in every way a contrast to the *Rosenkranzfest*. Dürer achieves an almost nightmare effect by compressing so much expression and gesture into so small an area. The picture is composed almost entirely of heads and hands, taken over directly from preliminary drawings (plate 32). According to the inscription, Dürer executed the work in five days and in parts the work is clearly unfinished. Conceivably Dürer realised that this lack of finish gave an added liveliness to the forms and that this led him to sign the picture prematurely. Dürer is said to have known of a picture by Leonardo of the same subject which inspired his work but there can have been very little actual resemblance between the two, although the contrast between youth and grotesque old age as shown in Dürer's picture was an idea which never ceased to fascinate Leonardo. On the other hand, it is not immediately apparent that Dürer's figure of Christ is not also a caricature. This effect cannot have been intentional but shows rather how Dürer was never really able to capture in paint Italian ideals of facial beauty. The figure of Christ is also an admirable illustration of Dürer's theory of consistency, that all the features of a given figure should agree in character and age. So here the hands of Christ are sharply contrasted with those of his interlocutors, just as their faces and expressions differ. It may seem no more than common sense that an artist should observe these distinctions but in Italy it was fairly common practice to make life studies for all the figures in a picture from studio apprentices and Dürer must have noticed inconsistencies in their finished works which would not have disturbed an Italian.

Dürer left Venice finally in 1507 and returned again to Nuremberg where he remained for the following thirteen years. During this period he produced few paintings for he was occupied with three series of woodcuts (two of which were begun before his departure), with major projects in engraving and experiments with allied techniques, and on time-absorbing commissions for the emperor Maximilian, whose service he entered in 1512. At the same time he began work on theoretical writings, a labour which continued until his death and covered an enormous range of subjects including the training of the artist, measurement, perspective, proportions and fortification.

A change appears in Dürer's woodcuts after his return home, and the scenes with which he completed *The Large Passion* and *The Life of the Virgin* (figure 4 on page 9) are altogether more atmospheric than the earlier prints, and show an extraordinary range in the densities of the shadows. The same is true of the post-Italian engravings (figure 6 on page 10) and Dürer is able by his handling of the light to evoke, even in small plates, effects of extraordinary density and monumentality in the figures. The engraving of *Christ presented to the People* of 1512 is one of the 16 scenes of *The Engraved Passion* (1506-13) which together with *The Small Woodcut Passion* with 25 scenes (1509-11) were Dürer's last series of prints. The two are executed in a similar format and show how carefully Dürer had calculated the potentialities of each medium. The woodcut of *Christ presented to the People* (figure 5 on page 10) is a scene of outwardly expressed emotion with a certain decorative ingredient in the design of the group of soldiers and even in the calligraphy of the lines, while the equivalent scene from *The Engraved Passion* (figure 6 on page 10) is composed of fewer and superbly massive figures whose feelings are expressed inwardly, with more dignity than abandon.

The major achievements in engraving at this time were, however, the three full plates known as the "Meisterstiche". The first of these (figure 11 on page 10), *The Knight, Death and Devil* (1513) is probably an allegory of Christianity, showing the Christian knight riding steadfastly past the threatening figures of death and the devil. The main figure is based on the drawing of 1498 (plate 6) but revised in the light of Dürer's knowledge of Italian equestrian sculptures, and so transformed from a study after nature to an engraved monument of the Christian faith. The second plate, of 1514, of *St Jerome in his Study* (figure 7 on page 10) shows the contemplative aspect of this faith. The print is in its way also a monument, but in the Flemish tradition, for it shows principally the interior of a room described in unusual detail and with an eye for effects of light and texture which could hardly be excelled even in paint. The third engraving (figure 8 on page 10), the "*Melancolia. I.*" of 1514, is perhaps Dürer's most famous work, and it is also one of his most obscure in subject. Every object in the picture probably has some hidden significance contributing to the theme of melancholy. If seen as a contrast to the other two subjects, the print takes on an additional significance, namely the futility of secular study, compared with the striking self-effacement and happy orderliness of the Christian contemplative or with purposeful progress of the active Christian. There is probably also a strong personal content in the "*Melancolia*" and the main figure, one feels, could quite easily have been a self-portrait (frontispiece). These three plates are linked not only in subject matter but also in the sense that each can be taken as a final statement of Dürer's skill as an engraver and his interest in engraving waned considerably after this supreme effort.

Painting was also gradually replaced by other pursuits but three major altarpieces occupied much of Dürer's time between 1508 and 1511. The first paintings produced after his return were the two life-size panels of *Adam and Eve* (plate 33) of 1507. It is perhaps significant, so shortly after Dürer's return from Venice, that his second statement of the subject should have been conceived in paint and in strikingly pictorial terms. The figures are less academically designed than in the early engraving (figure 3), and close in their instability and liveliness to German or Venetian rather than to classical sculpture. The movements of the figures are couched in flowing outlines: Adam gives the impression of having just arrived on the scene, breathless and with windblown hair, while Eve, in Dürer's preparatory drawings (figure 12 on page 11) was shown stretching upwards to pluck the apple in a pose of unusual exertion, and conceived as a silhouette bounded by a sinuous and almost uninterrupted contour line. It is not clear why the figures should have been painted on two panels (with slightly differing horizon lines) but they are linked visually by their glances and gestures and the action therefore appears to proceed from right to left across the two panels.

The first of Dürer's three altarpiece commissions, the *Martyrdom of the Ten Thousand Christians* (plate 34), was completed for Frederick the Wise of Saxony in 1508, as Dürer explains in his letters to Jacob Heller. The picture is an enlarged version in reverse of an earlier woodcut with a few additional groups of figures; in particular the three crosses in the right foreground and, in the centre, the figures of Dürer and a companion. It was not rare for artists to include concealed self-portraits in their major works and Dürer acquired this habit in the Job panels of about 1504 (see note to plate 17) but his later self-portraits are scarcely concealed. Here he strides forth in almost the very centre of the picture, dressed in his own clothes and apparently participating in the action of the picture as he is led by his companion towards a group which the latter points out with his right hand. As a curious conceit, the artist carries the picture's inscription on a banner, apparently improvised in the landscape from the branch of a tree.

The *Heller Altarpiece* is a more important work; but the central panel, which was executed by Dürer between 1508 and 1511, survives only in copies (plate 35), the original having been destroyed by fire in 1729. Ironically, copies of Dürer's letters to Heller about the work have also survived and they reveal much of interest about the artist, in particular his overriding obsession with the price of the picture, and about his working methods. When completed, the Heller altarpiece was, with the *Rosenkranzfest*, the most significant of Dürer's finished works. Both were large altarpieces with half life-size figures and the *Heller Altarpiece* with its more dramatic theme, the Assumption and Coronation of the Virgin, requiring as it did a large number of very active participants, must have presented to Dürer with greater force the problem of creating monumental figures in a clearly organised composition. This problem he has solved triumphantly. In contrast to his contemporary woodcut of the subject (figure 4), Dürer has filled most of the bottom half of the picture with the figures of only two of the apostles. They have the same prominence as the figures of the pope and the emperor in the *Rosenkranzfest* but they are more isolated from the groups to left and right and more convincing therefore as figures in the round. In conception and scale they have a greater monumentality and these qualities are conferred by implication on the smaller figures of the other apostles behind them.

The response of each figure to the scene they witness is carefully distinguished. The apostles are arranged in a convex group in depth, while a figure stooping to examine the grave fills the centre of a deep arc on the surface of the picture. The scene above them is designed to be complementary in pattern, with the cherubim spreading out the mantle of the Virgin in a concave silhouette. This mantle forms part of a pyramid in the overall design with its apex at the head of the Virgin and continues downwards through the upraised arms of the two kneeling apostles who flank the foreground. The figure of the Virgin is thus related visually to the apostles beneath, although the landscape and its horizon divides the picture in two zones. The figure of the artist can be seen in the distance in roughly the same position as in *The Martyrdom of the Ten Thousand Christians*, now holding a scroll with its inscription. Compared with Raphael's early picture of the subject of 1503 (figure 16 on page 12), Dürer's work has much of the formal counterpoint and magnificence of scale which are associated with the later works of Raphael, while at the same time it lacks none of Dürer's characteristic feeling for activity and excitement.

The third major altarpiece of this period is *The Adoration of the Trinity*, known as the *Allerheiligenbild*, of 1511 (plate 36). It was painted by Dürer for the chapel, dedicated to the Trinity and All Saints, of an almshouse in Nuremberg and the artist was also asked to design the windows of the chapel and the frame for its altarpiece. As early as 1508 he produced a water-colour sketch of the picture together with its frame (plate 37). This drawing not only reveals Dürer's knowledge of Renaissance architecture and his continuing interest in decorative ornament but, more significantly, it shows Dürer taking over and integrating with his picture a type of frame with a lunette supported on classical columns which had been much used by north Italian painters of the Renaissance. The columns flank the main picture and stabilise the composition while the frieze and the lunette above have a representation of the Last Judgment which were later executed in sculpture. The *Heller Altarpiece*, for all its modernity, formed part of a traditional triptych with folding wings, but Dürer conceived the *Allerheiligenbild* in a full Renaissance context. The picture survives today, out of its context, at Vienna. One can see how the subject has given Dürer little scope to develop further those principles found in the *Heller Altarpiece*. The composition is divided into tiers composed of relatively small figures, with representatives of mankind in order of precedence in the lowest zone and a portrait of Matthaeus Landauer, the founder of the almshouse, near the left-hand edge. In the next zone is a quorum of saints and above them angels spreading out the cloak of God the Father to reveal the figure of Christ on the cross. Higher still are cherubim and the dove of the Holy Ghost. Dürer himself stands in the landscape at the very bottom of the picture, watching the vision above and supporting a plaque with his signature and inscription.

Dürer was not to be commissioned with another altarpiece until shortly before his death and he produced very few paintings at all until after his journey to the Netherlands in 1520. One or two examples of his smaller religious works of this time show how consistently he maintained the general increase in the scale and bulk of his figures. In the *Virgin with the Pear* of 1512 (plate 38), the forms are almost as unbearably compressed as in the *Christ among the Doctors* of 1506. Little of the Virgin but her head appears as she looms forward from a dark background over the very fully modelled figure of the Christ child. As Dürer's output of paintings lessens so his style seems to become regressive. With *The Virgin in Prayer* of 1518 (plate 39), some of the timidity and fussiness of the early Dürer reappears. This is true also of the portrait of Wolgemut of 1516 (plate 40) with its flattened appearance and its emphasis on the lines and creases on the face and scrawny neck of the old painter.

Dürer was mainly occupied in the 1510s with work for the emperor Maximilian. Particularly time-consuming were two projects, a large triumphal arch, about ten feet square, executed on sixteen wood blocks and, with this, a woodcut triumphal procession measuring about sixty-five yards in length. Maximilian must have felt that Dürer, with his considerable knowledge of antiquity, was the artist best suited to carry out these extraordinary and bizarre commissions, devised by the humanists of his court as a suitably portable tribute to the king who has been described as the last of the knights-errant. Dürer's share in the actual work was relatively small; the designs for some parts were his and he supervised much of the execution. He left, however, two painted portraits of

22

the emperor, similar in design (plate 41) and both executed in 1519. They are elaborate and formalised half-lengths based on a drawing Dürer had made of the emperor in Augsburg in the previous year.

A smaller project for the emperor was the decoration of the margins of a printed prayer book with fanciful figure scenes and scrolls. Dürer drew forty-five of these sheets (plate 42) using one of three coloured inks for each, and it may have been intended to reprint the book with Dürer's decorations as an imitation manuscript. Each scene is loosely related to the text and the present illustration may have been suggested by a phrase in the accompanying Psalm. The drawings show an unusual side of Dürer's talent, an unflagging fantasy and wit which is only hinted at in his writings and rarely apparent in his other works.

On the other hand, these years were also ones of spiritual crisis for Dürer. Struggles with the papacy had begun in earnest in 1517. Dürer and his fellow townsmen were firmly on the side of Luther and the reformers and by 1524 the Reformation had been completed in Nuremberg. The strength of Dürer's faith in Luther is shown in the famous passage from his diary of the journey to the Netherlands when Dürer received the news of Luther's capture and wrote an intensely felt and moving record of his despair (see page 33). A similar sense of anguish can be traced in several graphic works produced in the mid-1510s, of which the most revealing is perhaps the etching of *The Agony in the Garden* of 1515 (figure 10 on page 11). Dürer probably turned to etching as a medium which is less controlled than engraving and capable of more dramatic linear patterns and brilliant contrasts of light and shade. So here Dürer expresses the sufferings of Christ in a way that can be paralleled only in the work of Grünewald, Dürer's contemporary and fellow-countryman. No direct contact between the two is recorded, except perhaps a brief meeting at Aachen in 1520, but Grünewald seems likewise to have been an active participant in the religious struggles of the time, which are powerfully reflected in his paintings.

In July 1520, Dürer left Nuremberg with his wife on a journey which lasted for over a year and took him across Germany and into the Netherlands. The main purpose of the journey was for Dürer to attend the coronation of the new emperor, Charles V, and renew his pension which had been in abeyance since the death of Maximilian in 1519. The journey, however, was also a pilgrimage to study the art treasures of the Netherlands, to distribute Dürer's own prints, to meet artists and patrons, and apparently also to see and acquire those rare curiosities so sought after by Dürer. In all these respects the journey was a triumph for the artist. His pension was renewed, he made friends with painters and patrons and was well received by all but the regent of the Netherlands herself. Dürer also made a special journey to see a whale which had been washed up on the coast of Zeeland, but arrived too late and contracted a malarial disease which slowly undermined his health, leading finally to his death at the age of 57 on 6 April 1528. There was, however, no abatement in Dürer's output during the last eight years of his life, although, to judge from the number of works which he left unfinished, his remarkable perseverance had also been undermined.

Dürer had little time for serious work in the Netherlands, but he filled at least one sketch book with a record of everything of interest, portraits and views in particular (figure 9 on page 11). The drawings are executed in silverpoint on prepared paper like the early *Self Portrait* (figure 1), and this apparently retrogressive technique must have seemed suitable for sketches which would have to be made in all conditions and with a minimum of preparation. Dürer also kept a famous journal of his daily activities, which is one of the most fascinating documents of the history of art. It is less revealing about his own work than some of the letters, but gives a clearer impression of the character of the author himself. In the fourteen years since his letters to Pirkheimer from Venice, Dürer's interests and his odd sense of priorities have scarcely changed. He was, however, more famous now and on a visit to a region where his work was more influential and better understood. This may account for the greater sense of self-assurance in the journal; but there is the same, seemingly petty-minded, concern for money, and an anxiety about being cheated and suffering indignities of other kinds.

There is a marked change in Dürer's style soon after his return from the Netherlands in 1521 which continues until his death seven years later. This cannot be ascribed to the influence of Netherlandish art, although it may have been in part a reaction to it, for Dürer moves in the opposite direction, his works becoming more simplified and classical. Like the great last phase of many another creative genius, Dürer's late style emerges rather unexpectedly and its fruits are often experimental in character and quintessential in their clarity and directness.

Portraits played a large part in Dürer's output at this time. In the Netherlands he won recognition for drawings as an acceptable form of portraiture and many were quick to take advantage of so cheap and rapid a medium. Dürer continued to produce highly finished presentation drawings of this kind even after he had returned to Nuremberg (plate 46). Painted portraits are also numerous. The *Unknown Man* of 1524 (plate 43) is one of the last and most splendid examples in Dürer's well-established portrait convention. The *Hieronymus Holzschuher* of two years later (plate 44), however, creates a different effect. As though it were a self-portrait, the eyes gaze directly out, while the face is turned to the right. The picture has a pendant in the more conventional portrait of Jacob Muffel, and Dürer may have intended to link the two pictures by making Holzschuher glance round towards his companion, but he gives the sitter a florid and unguarded appearance as he confronts the spectator face to face.

From the same year, 1526, dates the extraordinary *Portrait of Johannes Kleberger* (plate 45) which is conceived as a classical portrait head in an inscribed and coloured roundel. Renaissance artists like Mantegna had already adapted this Roman architectural motif in painting, but Dürer seems to have been the first to use it for an actual portrait. Dürer cannot, however, avoid bringing the bodyless head to life; it is fully modelled in colour and observed in as great detail as his more conventional portraits, and like them it shows, for example, the lights of a window reflected on the surface of each eye. The effect is therefore of an uneasy compromise between Dürer's instinctive leaning towards naturalistic detail and a self-imposed classical ideal. It may, however, be that Dürer had some knowledge of the work of contemporary Italian artists who were experimenting with similar but apparently wilful confusions of the real and the unreal in their pictures; such ambiguities were also found in German art at this time, notably in the work of Grünewald. The drawn *Portrait of Ulrich Starck* (plate 46) also derives ultimately from Roman portraits, but the profile view has prevented Dürer from enlivening the face with any strong expression and seen from below the sitter attains the true *gravitas* of his Roman predecessors.

This new classical ideal can also be felt in the last religious works of the artist, for example, in his superb drawing of 1527 which shows *The Annunciation* in pen and water-colour (plate 47). Perhaps an even better illustration of this change in Dürer's style is the slightly earlier drawing of 1524 of *The Adoration of the Kings* (figure 13 on page 12). It is one of many oblong scenes of the Passion story which were probably intended as studies for a set of woodcuts of which only *The Last Supper* was actually cut. The present scene resembles a sculptural relief, an effect suggested by the oblong shape with the figures arranged in a row in the foreground. The pen technique, which Dürer had employed occasionally since the 1510s, with parallel lines of hatchings hardly ever curved and seldom crossing, gives the forms a faceted simplicity. This change can be clearly felt by comparing Dürer's picture of 1504 (plate 17) and even the expressions and gestures of the participants are now more discreet and formal. In engraving, Dürer began a set of single figures of apostles, unusually austere in design, but his main work was an elaborate *Crucifixion* which was not completed although a number of studies for it survive, like the metalpoint drawing of *Christ on the Cross* of 1523 (plate 48). The figure is softly modelled in great detail but the overall effect is one of monumental simplicity and firmness, with each foot nailed separately on the cross.

Dürer's major work in painting was a large altarpiece for which many studies exist but which was never carried out in paint, except perhaps for one of the wings. For the two pictures of four saints presented by Dürer to the city of Nuremberg in 1526 (plate 50) may actually have originated as part of this altarpiece, being later adapted for presentation. The centre panel (figure 14 on page 12) was conceived in 1521-2 as a pure "sacra conversazione" with the figures of saints standing around the enthroned Virgin and Child in the centre. The theme is compatible with the aims of Dürer's late style and he seems to have developed the composition with unprecedented thoroughness, for there exist, in addition to carefully-finished drawings for the individual figures, at least four rough studies of experiments for the group as a whole, even with the colours fully worked out as in the present example. The resulting painting would certainly have been comparable to the *Heller Altarpiece* but there is no dramatic theme, no cherubim, hardly any landscape — the picture would have depended entirely for its effect on the grouping of the figures and their monumental conception.

Some idea of what the central group would have looked like if brought to life in paint can be gained from Dürer's last small Madonna (plate 49) of 1526 with its almost hieratic simplicity and reserve. There is little communication between the two figures here, compared with the composition of 1512 (plate 38), and they are visually so far apart that the picture looks almost like a fragment, as though Dürer had been thinking in the larger terms of his "sacra conversazione" when painting this little scene. A clear impression of the magisterial scale and conception of the figures surrounding the Virgin and Child is given by the two wings of 1526 (plate 50). The saints here resemble sculptures emerging from the block, for they are packed densely into dark and narrow compartments and make their impact largely by means of the brilliantly coloured and lit, and seemingly carved, drapery which envelopes them. Although they derive from Bellini, Dürer's own late and austere engravings of the apostles are closer in character and in scale and a revealing comparison with Michelangelo has also been suggested.

In spite of their apparent directness, however, these figures also embody those universal symbols so essential to Dürer, for each saint represents one of the four temperaments and one of the four ages of man according to his temperament. The two panels may also contrast the contemplative and active life. Finally, Dürer appends at the bottom of the picture an excerpt from the writings of each saint in the Lutheran translation of the Bible in what amounts to a personal statement of his own convictions. The picture is significant, therefore, not only as a measure of Dürer's many-sided artistic genius, but as a symbol also of his whole intellectual achievement, which is expressed so ably in Dürer's own writings.

The following quotations from Dürer's writings have been taken from W. M. Conway, *Literary Remains of Albrecht Dürer*, Cambridge University Press, 1889. Erwin Panofsky's *The Life and Art of Albrecht Dürer*, Oxford University Press, 1945, is indispensable for a full understanding of the artist and contains a selected bibliography.

FROM THE FAMILY HISTORY WRITTEN BY DÜRER IN 1524

So Albrecht Dürer, my dear father, came to Germany. He had been a long time with the great artists in the Netherlands. At last he came hither to Nuremberg in the year, as reckoned from the birth of Christ, 1455, on St Eulogius' day. And on the same day Philip Pirkheimer had his marriage feast at the Veste, and there was a great dance under the big lime tree. For a long time after that, my dear father, Albrecht Dürer, served my grandfather, old Hieronymus Holper, till the year reckoned 1467 after the birth of Christ. My grandfather than gave him his daughter, a pretty upright girl, fifteen years old, named Barbara; and he was wedded to her eight days before St Vitus'.

This my dear Father was very careful with his children to bring them up in the fear of God; for it was his highest wish to train them well that they might be pleasing in the sight both of God and man. Wherefore his daily speech to us was that we should love God and deal truly with our neighbours.

And my Father took special pleasure in me because he saw that I was diligent in striving to learn. So he sent me to the school, and when I had learnt to read and write he took me away from it, and taught me the goldsmith's craft. But when I could work neatly my liking drew me rather to painting than to goldsmith's work, so I laid it before my father; but he was not well pleased, regretting the time lost while I had been learning to be a goldsmith. Still he let it be as I wished, and in 1486 (reckoned from the birth of Christ) on St Andrew's day my Father bound me apprentice to Michael Wolgemut, to serve him three years long. During that time God gave me diligence so that I learnt well, but I had much to suffer from his lads.

When I had finished my learning, my Father sent me off, and I stayed away four years till he called me back again. As I had gone forth in the year 1490 after Easter, so now I came back again in 1494, as it is reckoned, after Whitsuntide.

When I returned home Hans Frey treated with my Father, and gave me his daughter, Mistress Agnes by name, and with her he gave me 200 florins, and we were wedded; it was on Monday before Margaret's in the year 1494.

Some time after it happened that my father was so ill with dysentery that no one could stop it. And when he saw death before his eyes, he gave himself willingly to it, with great patience, and he commended my mother to me, and exhorted me to live in a manner pleasing to God. He received the Holy Sacraments and passed away Christianly (as I have described at length in another book) in the year 1502, after midnight before St Matthew's eve. God be gracious and merciful to him.

Two years after my Father's death I took my Mother into my house, for she had nothing more to live upon. So she dwelt with me till the year 1513, as they reckon it; when, early one Tuesday morning, she was taken suddenly and deadly ill, and thus she lay a whole year long. And a whole year after the day she was first taken ill, she received the holy sacraments and Christianly passed away two hours before nightfall — it was on a Friday, the 17th day of May in the year 1514. I said the prayers for her myself. God Almighty be gracious to her.

FROM THE LETTERS OF 1506 WRITTEN TO PIRKHEIMER FROM VENICE

How I wish you were here at Venice! There are so many nice men among the Italians who seek my company more and more every day—which is very pleasing to one—men of sense and knowledge, good lute-players and pipers, judges of painting, men of much noble sentiment and honest virtue, and they show me much honour and friendship. On the other hand there are also amongst them some of the most false, lying, thievish rascals; I should never have believed that such were living in the world. If one did not know them, one would think them the nicest men the earth could show.

The painters here, let me tell you, are very unfriendly to me. They have summoned me three times before the magistrates and I have had to pay four florins to their school. You must also know that I might have gained a great deal of money if I had not undertaken to paint the German picture. There is much work in it and I cannot get it quite finished before Whitsuntide. Yet they only pay me 85 ducats for it. Now you know how much it costs to live, and then I have bought some things and sent some money away, so that I have not much before me now. But don't misunderstand me, I am firmly purposed not to go away hence till God enables me to repay you with thanks and to have a hundred florins over besides. I should easily earn this if I had not got the German picture to paint, for all men except the painters wish me well.

For one thing I return you my thanks, namely for explaining my position in the best way to my wife; but I know that there is no lack of wisdom in you. If only you had my meekness you would have all virtues. Thank you also for all the good you have done me, if only you would not bother me about the rings! If they don't please you break their heads off and pitch them out on to the dunghill as Peter Weisweber says. What do you mean by setting me to such dirty work? I have become a *gentleman* at Venice.

My picture (plate 27), you must know, says it would give a ducat for you to see it, it is well painted and beautifully coloured. I have earned much praise but little profit by it. In the time it took to paint I could easily have earned 220 ducats, and now I have declined much work, in order that I may come home. I have stopped the mouths of all the painters who used to say that I was good at engraving but, as to painting, I did not know how to handle my colours. Now everyone says that better colouring they have never seen.

You must know that my picture is finished as well as another *Quadro* the like of which I have never painted before (plate 31?). And as you are so pleased with yourself, let me tell you that there is no better Madonna picture in the land than mine; for all the painters praise it, as the nobles do you. They say that they have never seen a nobler, more charming painting, and so forth.

In reply to your question when I shall come home, I tell you, so that my lords may also make their arrangements, that I shall have finished here in ten days; after that I should like to ride to Bologna to learn the secrets of the art of perspective, which a man is willing to teach me. I should stay there eight or ten days and then return to Venice. After that I shall come with the next messenger. How I shall freeze after this sun! Here I am a gentleman, at home only a parasite.

FROM THE LETTERS OF 1507-1509 TO JACOB HELLER

First, my willing service to you, dear Herr Heller. I was pleased to get your kind letter. You must know, however, that I have been for a long time plagued with a fever, which has thrown me back some weeks in my work for Duke Frederick of Saxony (plate 34), and has caused me great loss. But now I mean to finish my work for him quickly, for it is more than half done. So have patience with me about your picture, which, as soon as I get this work finished to the satisfaction of the above mentioned Prince, I will at once set myself diligently to paint, as I promised you here.

And although I have not yet begun on the panel, I have got it from the joiner and have paid away for it the money you gave me. He would not lower his price for it, though I thought he did not deserve so much. I have given it to a preparer who has whitened it and painted it and will put on the gilding next week.

Dear Herr Jacob Heller, in a fortnight I shall be ready with Duke Frederick's work after that I shall begin yours (plate 35), and, as my custom is, I will not paint any other picture till it is finished. I will be sure carefully to paint the middle panel with my own hand; apart from that, the outer sides of the wings are already sketched in — they will be in stone colour; I have also had the ground laid. So much for news.

I wish you could see my gracious Lord's picture; I think it would please you. I have worked at it straight on for a year and gained very little by it; for I only get 280 Rhenish gulden for it, and I have spent all that in the time. And so I say if I do not paint your picture to your perfect satisfaction, no man shall persuade me to make a bargain for anything again, for I neglect better chances by so doing...

Dear Herr Jacob, I have safely received your letter, that is to say the last but one, and I gather from it that you wish me to make you a good picture, which is just what I myself have in mind to do. You must know how far it has got on; the wings have been painted in stone colours on the outside, but they are not yet varnished; inside the whole of the ground has been laid, so that it is ready to paint on.

The middle panel I have outlined with the greatest care and at cost of much time; it is also laid over with two very good colours upon which I can begin to paint the ground. For I intend, so soon as I hear that you approve, to paint the ground some four, five, or six times over, for clearness' and durability's sake, using the very best Ultramarine for the purpose that I can get. And no one shall paint a stroke on it except myself...

Now I commend myself to you. I want you also to know that in all my days I have never begun any work that pleased me better than this picture of yours which I am painting. Till I finish it I will not do any other work; I am only sorry that the winter will so soon come upon me. The days grow so short that one cannot do much.

I would not paint another like it for three times the price agreed, for I neglect myself for it, suffer loss, and earn anything but thanks from you.

I am using, let me tell you, quite the finest colours I can get. Of ultramarine I shall want 20 ducats' worth alone, not counting the other expenses. When the picture is once finished I am quite sure that you yourself will say that anything more beautiful you have never seen; but I dare not expect from beginning to end to finish the painting of the middle panel in less than thirteen months. I shall not begin any other work till it is finished, though it will be much to my hurt. Then what do you suppose my expenses will be while I am working at it? You would not undertake to keep me for that time for 200 florins. Only think what you have repeatedly written about the materials. If you wanted to buy a pound of Ultramarine you would hardly get it for 100 florins, for I cannot buy an ounce of it good for less than 10 or 12 ducats...

You further reproach me with having promised you, that I would paint your picture with the greatest possible care that ever I could. That I certainly never said or if I did I was out of my senses, for in my whole life-time I should scarcely finish it. With such extraordinary care I can hardly finish a face in half a year; now your picture contains fully 100 faces, not reckoning the drapery and landscape, and other things in it. Besides who ever heard of making such a work for an altarpiece? No one could see it. But I think it was thus that I wrote to you — that I would paint the picture with great or more than ordinary pains because of the time which you waited for me.

First my willing service to you, dear Herr Jacob Heller. In accordance with your last letter I am sending the picture well packed and seen to in all needful points...

If it is kept clean I know it will remain bright and fresh 500 years, for it is not done as men are wont to paint. So have it kept clean and don't let it be touched or sprinkled with holy water. I feel sure it will not be criticised, or only for the purpose of annoying me; and I answer for it; it will please you well...

30

But very careful nicety does not pay. So henceforth I shall stick to my engraving, and had I done so before I should today have been a richer man by 1000 florins...

If anyone wants to see it, let it hang forward two or three finger breadths, for then the light is good to see it by. And when I come over to you, say in one, two, or three years' time, if the picture is properly dry, it must be taken down and I will varnish it over anew with some excellent varnish, which no one else can make; it will then last 100 years longer than it would before. But don't let anybody else varnish it, for all other varnishes are yellow, and the picture would be ruined for you. And if a thing, on which I have spent more than a year's work, were ruined it would be grief to me. When you have it set up be present yourself to see that it gets no harm. Deal carefully with it, for you will hear from your own and from foreign painters how it is done.

FROM A LETTER PROBABLY OF 1520 TO GEORG SPALATIN, CHAPLAIN TO DUKE FREDERICK OF SAXONY

God helping me, if ever I meet Dr Martin Luther, I intend to draw a careful portrait of him from the life and to engrave it on copper, for a lasting remembrance of a Christian man who helped me out of great distress. And I beg your worthiness to send me for my money anything new that Dr Martin may write...

With this letter I send for my most gracious lord three impressions of a copper-plate of my most gracious lord of Mainz, which I engraved at his request. I sent the copper-plate with 200 impressions as a present to his Electoral Grace, and he graciously sent me in return 200 florins in gold and 20 ells of damask for a coat. I joyfully and thankfully accepted them, especially as I was in want of them at that time.

FROM THE DIARY OF THE JOURNEY TO THE NETHERLANDS, JULY 1520—JULY 1521

On Thursday after Kilian's, I, Albrecht Dürer, at my own charges and costs, took myself and my wife (and maid Susanna) away to the Netherlands...

At Antwerp I went to Jobst Plankfelt's inn, and the same evening the Fuggers' Factor, Bernhard Stecher, invited me and gave us a costly meal...

On Sunday, it was St Oswald's day, the painters invited me to the hall of their guild, with my wife and maid. All their service was of silver, and they had other splendid ornaments and very costly meats. All their wives also were there. And as I was being led to the table the company stood on both sides as if they were leading some great lord. And there were amongst them men of very high position, who all behaved most respectfully towards me with deep courtesy, and promised to do everything in their power agreeable to me that they knew of. And as I was sitting there in such honour the Syndic of Antwerp came, with two servants, and presented me with four cans of wine in the name of the Town Councillors of Antwerp, and they had bidden him say that they wished thereby to show their respect for me and to assure me of their good will...

In the golden chamber in the Townhall at Brussels I saw the four paintings which the great Master Roger van der Weyden made. And I saw out behind the King's house at Brussels the fountains, labyrinth, and Beast-garden; anything more beautiful and pleasing to me and more like a Paradise I have never seen. Erasmus is the name of the little man who wrote out my supplication at Herr Jacob de Bannisis' house. At Brussels is a very splendid Townhall, large, and covered with beautiful carved stonework, and it has a noble, open tower. I took a portrait at night by candlelight of Master Konrad of Brussels, who was my host: I drew at the same time Doctor Lamparter's son in charcoal, also the hostess.

I saw the things which have been brought to the King from the new land of gold (Mexico), a sun all of gold a whole fathom broad, and a moon all of silver of the same size, also two rooms full of the armour of the people there, and all manner of wondrous weapons of theirs, harness and darts, very strange clothing, beds, and all kinds of wonderful objects of human use, much better worth seeing than prodigies. These things were all so precious that they are valued at 100,000 florins. All the days of my life I have seen nothing that rejoiced my heart so much as these things, for I saw amongst them wonderful works of art, and I marvelled at the subtle *Ingenia* of men in foreign lands. Indeed I cannot express all that I thought there...

At Antwerp Again:

The studio of Raphael of Urbino has quite broken up since his death, but one of his scholars, Tommaso Vincidor of Bologna by name, a good painter, desired to see me. So he came to me and has given me an antique gold ring with a very well cut stone. It is worth 5 fl. but already I have been offered the double for it. I gave him 6 fl. worth of my best prints for it...

On Monday after Michaelmas 1520, I gave Thomas of Bologna a whole set of prints to send for me to Rome to another painter who should send me Raphael's work in return...

Visit to Zeeland:

From thence I went to Middelburg. There, in the Abbey, is a great picture painted by Jan de Mabuse — not so good in the modelling as in the colouring. I went next to the Veere, where lie ships from all lands; it is a very fine little town.

At Arnemuiden, where I landed before, a great misfortune befell me. As we were pushing ashore and getting out our rope, a great ship bumped hard against us, as we were in the act of landing, and in the crush I had let every one get out before me, so that only I, Georg Koetzler, two old wives, and the skipper with a small boy were left in the ship. When now the other ship bumped against us, and I with those named was still in the ship and could not get out, the strong rope broke; and thereupon, in the same moment, a storm of wind arose, which drove our ship back with force. Then we all cried for help but no one would risk himself for us. And the wind carried us away, out to sea. Thereupon the skipper tore his hair and cried aloud, for all his men had landed and the ship was unmanned. Then were we in fear and danger, for the wind was strong and only six persons in the ship. So I spoke to the skipper that he should take courage and have hope in God, and that he should consider what was to be done. So he said that if he could haul up the small sail he would try if we could come again to land. So we toiled all together and got it feebly about halfway up, and went on again towards the land. And when the people on shore, who had already given us up, saw how we helped ourselves, they came to our aid and we got to land.

Middelburg is a good town; it has a very beautiful Townhall with a fine tower. There is much art shown in all things here. In the Abbey the stalls are very costly and beautiful, and there is a splendid gallery of stone; and there is a fine Parish Church. The town was besides excellent for sketching...

Early on Monday we started again by ship and went by the Veere and Zierikzee and tried to get sight of the great fish but the tide had carried him off again...

Visit to Bruges and Ghent:

When I reached Bruges Jan Prost took me in to lodge in his house and prepared the same night a costly meal and bade much company to meet me. Next day Marx, the goldsmith, invited me and gave me a costly meal and asked many to meet me. Afterwards they took me to see the Emperor's house which is large and splendid. I saw the chapel there which Roger (Rogier van der Weyden) painted, and some pictures by a great old master; I gave 1 st. to the man who showed us them. Then I bought 3 ivory combs for 30 st. They took me next to St Jacob's and showed me the precious pictures by Roger and Hugo (Hugo van der Goes), who were both great masters. Then I saw in our Lady's Church the alabaster Madonna, sculptured by Michelangelo of Rome. After that they took me to many more churches and showed me all the good pictures, of which there is an abundance there; and when I had seen the Jan van Eyck and all the other works, we came at last to the painters' chapel, in which there are good things. Then they prepared a banquet for me, and I went with them from it to their guild-hall, where many honourable men were gathered together, both goldsmiths, painters and merchants, and they made me sup with them. They gave me presents, sought to make my acquaintance, and did me great honour.

At Antwerp Again:

In the third week after Easter a violent fever seized me, with great weakness, nausea, and headache. And before, when I was in Zeeland, a wondrous sickness overcame me, such as I never heard of from any man, and this sickness remains with me.

On Friday before Whitsunday in the year 1521, came tidings to me at Antwerp, that Martin Luther had been so treacherously taken prisoner; for he trusted the Emperor Karl, who had granted him his herald and imperial safe-conduct. But as soon as the herald had conveyed him to an unfriendly place near Eisenach he rode away, saying that he no longer needed him. Straightway there appeared ten knights and they treacherously carried off the pious man, betrayed into their hands, a man enlightened by the Holy Ghost, a follower of the true Christian faith. And whether he yet lives I know not, or whether they have put him to death; if so, he has suffered for the truth of Christ and because he rebuked the unchristian Papacy, which strives with its heavy load of human laws against the redemption of Christ. And if he has suffered it is that we may again be robbed and stripped of the fruit of our blood and sweat, that the same may be shamefully and scandalously squandered by idle-going folk, while the poor and the sick therefore die of hunger. But this is above all most grievous to me, that, may be, God will suffer us to remain still longer under their false, blind doctrine, invented and drawn up by the men alone whom they call Fathers, by whom also the precious Word of God is in many places wrongly expounded or utterly ignored...

Oh all ye pious Christian men, help me deeply to bewail this man, inspired of God, and to pray Him yet again to send us an enlightened man.

Visit to Lady Margaret, the Regent of the Netherlands, at Mechlin:

And I went to Lady Margaret's and showed her my *Emperor*, and would have presented it to her, but she so disliked it that I took it away with me.

And on Friday Lady Margaret showed me all her beautiful things, amongst them I saw about 40 small oil pictures, the like of which for precision and excellence I have never beheld. There also I saw more good works by Jan de Mabuse and Jacob Walch (Jacopo de' Barbari). I asked my Lady for Jacob's little book, but she said she had already promised it to her painter. Then I saw many other costly things and a precious library.

FROM LETTERS OF 1524 AND 1526 TO THE TOWN COUNCIL OF NUREMBERG

Again, nineteen years ago, the government of Venice offered to appoint me to an office and to give me a salary of 200 ducats a year. So too, only a short time ago when I was in the Netherlands, the Council of Antwerp would have given me 300 Philipsgulden a year, kept me there free of taxes, and honoured me with a well-built house; and besides I should have been paid in addition at both places for all the work I might have done for the gentry. But I declined all this, because of the particular love and affection which I bear to your honourable Wisdoms and to my fatherland, this honourable town, preferring, as I did, to live under your Wisdoms in a moderate way rather than to be rich and held in honour in other places...

Prudent, honourable, wise, dear Masters. I have been intending, for a long time past, to show my respect for your Wisdoms by the presentation of some humble picture of mine as a remembrance; but I have been prevented from so doing by the imperfection and insignificance of my works, for I felt that with such I could not well stand before your Wisdoms. Now, however, that I have just painted a panel (plate 50) upon which I have bestowed more trouble than on any other painting, I considered none more worthy to keep it as a reminiscence than your Wisdoms...

FROM DÜRER'S INSCRIPTION ON HIS PICTURE OF "THE FOUR APOSTLES" (plate 50)

All wordly rulers in these dangerous times should give heed that they receive not human misguidance for the Word of God, for God will have nothing added to His Word nor taken away from it. Hear therefore these four excellent men, Peter, John, Paul and Mark, their warning...

34

FROM MISCELLANEOUS WRITINGS ON ART
(Fragments of a general treatise)

Now I know that in our German nation, at the present time, are many painters who stand in need of instruction, for they lack all real art, yet they nevertheless have many great works to make. Forasmuch then as they are so numerous, it is very needful for them to learn to better their work...

Every form brought before our vision falleth upon it as upon a mirror. We regard a form and figure out of nature with more pleasure than any other, though the thing in itself is not necessarily altogether better or worse. We like to behold beautiful things, for it is pleasant to us to criticise; and Beauty is more credible in a skilful painter's work than in another's. True proportion maketh a good figure both in painting and in all arts. I shall not labour in vain if I set down that which may be useful for painting. For the art of painting is employed in the service of the Church and by it the sufferings of Christ and many other profitable examples are set forth. It preserveth also the likeness of men after their death. By aid of delineations the measurements of the earth, the waters, and the stars are better to be understood; and many things likewise become known unto men by them. The attainment of true, artistic, and lovely execution in painting is hard to come unto; it needeth long time and a hand practised to almost perfect freedom. Whosoever, therefore, falleth short of this cannot attain a right understanding (in matters of painting) for it cometh alone by inspiration from above. The art of painting cannot be truly judged save by such as are themselves good painters; from others verily is it hidden even as a strange tongue. It were a noble occupation for ingenious youths without employment to exercise themselves in this art...

Many hundred years ago there were still some famous painters, such as those named Phidias, Praxiteles, Apelles, Polycleitus, Parrhasius, Lysippus, Protogenes, and the rest, some of whom wrote about their art and very artfully described it and gave it plainly to the light; but their praiseworthy books are, so far, unknown to us, and perhaps have been altogether lost by war, driving forth of the peoples, and alterations of laws and beliefs — a loss much to be regretted by every wise man. It often came to pass that noble *Ingenia* were destroyed by barbarous oppressors of art; for if they saw figures traced in few lines they thought it nought but vain, devilish sorcery. And in destroying them they attempted to honour God by something displeasing to him; and, to use the language of men, God was angry with all destroyers of the works of great mastership, which is only attained by much toil, labour, and expenditure of time, and is bestowed by God alone. Often do I sorrow because I must be robbed of the aforesaid Masters' books of art; but the enemies of art despise these things.

FROM THE DEDICATION TO "THE TEACHING OF MEASUREMENTS," 1525

To my very dear Master and friend, Herr Willibald Pirkheimer, I, Albrecht Dürer, wish health and happiness.

Gracious Master and friend. Heretofore many talented scholars in our German land have been taught the art of painting, without any foundation and almost according to mere every-day rule-of-thumb. Thus they have grown up in ignorance, like a wild unpruned tree. And, though some of them have acquired a free hand by continuous practice, so that it cannot be denied that their work has been done skilfully, yet, instead of being grounded upon principle, it has merely been made according to their tastes. If, however, painters of understanding and artists worthy of the name were to see so rash a work, they would scorn the blindness of these fellows, and that not without justice. For, to one who really knows, nothing is more unpleasant to see in a picture than fundamental error, however carefully the details may be painted. That such painters have found satisfaction in their errors is only because they have not learnt the *Art of Measurement*, without which no one can either be or become a master of his craft. But that again has been the fault of their masters, who themselves were ignorant of this art.

FROM THE DEDICATION TO "THE FOUR BOOKS OF HUMAN PROPORTION", 1528

That must be a strangely dull head which never trusts itself to find out anything fresh but only travels along the old path, simply following others and not daring to reflect, for itself. For it beseems each Understanding, in following another, not to despair of, itself also, discovering something better. If that is done, there remaineth no doubt but that, in time, this Art will again reach the perfection it attained amongst the Ancients. For it is evident that, though the German painters are not a little skilful with the hand and in the use of colours, they have as yet been wanting in the arts of measurement, perspective, and other like matters. It is therefore to be hoped that, if they learn these also and gain skill by knowledge and knowledge by skill, they will in time allow no other nation to take the prize before them.

Notes on the Plates

Plate 1 *Portrait of Dürer's Father*. Monogram and date, 1490 (added later?). Oil on wood. 48⁵/₁₆ × 36¹/₁₆ in. (123 × 890 cm.). Florence, Galleria degli Uffizi.

This portrait is not only Dürer's earliest but apparently also his largest. The rosary in the hands of the sitter confirms the impression given by Dürer in his family chronicle of the striking piety of his father. Painted on the reverse of the panel are the arms of both of Dürer's parents and the present picture may have been a pendant to a now lost portrait of his mother. There are versions of a second picture of the father, painted probably about 1497 (London, National Gallery, see note to Pl. 20), but the appearance of the mother is known only from a superb chalk drawing (Berlin) made in 1514 just before her death. Likewise known from drawings are the features of Dürer's wife and of one of his brothers. This gallery of family portraits is in its conception very much a part of Dürer's precocious urge for self-documentation as expressed in his family chronicle and, of course, in his own self-portraits.

Plate 2 *The Wire-Drawing Mill*. Monogram, added later. Probably 1489. Water-colour and gouache. 11¹/₄ × 16³/₄ in. (28.6 × 42.6 cm.). Inscribed: "trotzeihmüll". Berlin-Dahlem, Staatliche Museen. Kupferstichkabinett.

One of a group of about six water-colours of landscape or of trees made in the months immediately preceding Dürer's departure from Nuremberg in 1490. The topographical accuracy of the present study can be tested in comparison with a later chalk drawing (Bayonne) made by Dürer about 1517 of the same place and the principal difference between the two drawings lies not in the content of the scene but in the character of the representation. The earlier study is seen from a high viewpoint (and hence resembles a detail of the background of a painting) but Dürer gradually approaches closer to the subject (Pls. 10 and 11) and in his later sketch of the wire-drawing mill the buildings loom prominently

in the foreground, overshadowing the horizon and taking a more active part in the composition of the picture.

Plate 3 *Self Portrait*. Inscribed and dated 1493. Oil on vellum, transferred to canvas. 22¹/₄ × 17¹/₂ in. (56.5 × 44.5 cm.). Paris, Musée du Louvre.

In this, the first of Dürer's painted self-portraits, the convincing anatomical structure of the figure has already been stressed. However, it seems to be based in pose and dress on a drypoint engraving executed by the Hausbuch Master, an artist in whom the young Dürer took an especial interest and who may have attracted him to the Rhine area or Holland at the beginning of his "bachelor journey". It has also been noticed that Dürer had some difficulty in introducing his own right hand into the picture, where it appears as the left hand plucking rather unconvincingly at the stem of the flower which he holds. In the early self-portrait (Fig. 1) and the third painted self-portrait (Pl. 21) this hand is simply concealed.

Plates 4 and 5 *Arco*. Probably 1495. Water-colour and gouache. 8¹¹/₁₆ × 8¹¹/₁₆ in. (22.1 × 22.1 cm.). Inscribed: "Fenedier klawsen", with monogram (added later?). Paris, Louvre. *Alpine Landscape*. Probably 1495. Water-colour and gouache. 8⁵/₁₆ × 12³/₈ in. (21.2 × 31.4 cm.). Inscribed: "wehlschperg". Oxford, Ashmolean Museum.

Two of about ten water-colour landscapes executed in the Alps, probably on the return journey from Venice in the spring of 1495. The extreme bravura of the second example has suggested to some critics that it was made on the second trip to Venice ten years later but it seems improbable that only one such water-colour should have survived from his second journey. The fascination of the Alps for Northern artists is shown also in the multitude of very different drawings by Peter Brueghel executed in the 1550s, and in the works of a handful of Flemish artists working later in the century, the so-called "Frankenthal" school.

Plate 6 *Soldier on Horseback*. Inscribed, with monogram and date, 1498 (added later?). Pen and water-colour. $16^1/_4 \times 12^3/_4$ in. (41 × 32.4 cm.). Vienna, Albertina.

The present drawing can be compared with Dürer's later interpretations of the horse, his two engravings of 1505 and the *Knight, Death and Devil* of 1513 (Fig. 11), where the influence of Leonardo and of Italian sculptural monuments (in particular, the bronze horses of St Mark's) entirely altered Dürer's conception of the animal. A legend has it that the sitter in this drawing is a groom of the Paumgärtner family, and its date, 1498, is the same as the traditional date of the Paumgärtner altarpiece (Pl. 14). At least one critic has doubted the authenticity of the drawing.

Plate 7 *Nuremberg Woman dressed for Church*. Inscribed, with monogram and date, 1500. Pen and water-colour. $12^5/_8 \times 8^1/_{16}$ in. (32 × 20.5 cm.). Vienna, Albertina.

One of a group of some five water-colour studies of about 1500 of the dress worn for different occasions by the towns-women of Nuremberg. In Venice in 1494, Dürer had made a witty pen sketch in which he compared the clothes of a Venetian and a Nuremberg woman, much apparently to the disadvantage of the latter, who looks with a seemingly jealous amazement at the taller and grander figure of her companion. A lively interest in clothes is fully revealed in Dürer's letters and in other drawings produced sporadically throughout his career.

Plate 8 *Lobster*. Monogram and date, 1495. Pen on brown prepared paper with brown and black washes, heightened with white. $9^7/_{16} \times 16^{15}/_{16}$ in. (24.3 × 43 cm.). Berlin-Dahlem, Staatliche Museen, Kupferstichkabinett.

Two aspects of Dürer's taste are combined in this early drawing, his unusual interest in animals and more particularly a fascination for rare and grotesque species, which is manifest in later works like the drawing of a walrus (British Museum) or the famous woodcut based on a description of a rhinocerous. This same curiosity moved Dürer to make his futile excursion to Zeeland in 1521 to see a whale which had been washed ashore there.

Plate 9 *Young Hare*. Monogram and date, 1502. Water-colour and gouache. $9^7/_8 \times 8^7/_8$ in. (25.1 × 22.6 cm.). Vienna, Albertina.

Dürer's detailed water-colours of animals and plants have long been regarded as his most attractive productions and have given rise to more imitations than any other branch of his work. Most of the authentic drawings, like the present example or the roughly contemporary *Large piece of Turf*

(Albertina) correspond with a phase in Dürer's career in the early 1500s when maximum detail was regarded as a prerequisite in all his works. It can be traced, for example, in the engravings (Fig. 3) as well as in the paintings (Pl. 17) of these years.

Plates 10 and 11 *House on an Island in a Pond*. Probably 1495/7. Water-colour and gouache. $8^3/_8 \times 8^3/_4$ in. (21.3 × 22.2 cm.). Inscribed: "weier Haws", with monogram (added later?). London, British Museum. *Pond in the Woods*. ("Morgendämmerung"). Water-colour and gouache. $10^5/_{16} \times 14^3/_4$ in. (26.2 × 37.4 cm.). Monogram. London, British Museum.

Dürer made about a dozen water-colours of Nuremberg and neighbouring areas in the years immediately following his return from Venice in 1495. Many of them are of quarries, a subject which he may have considered a local substitute for the Alps. His water-colour landscapes are a curiously isolated phenomenon and few, if any, contemporary artists shared Dürer's enthusiasm. Despite the growing interest in landscape with the slightly later group of German painters, the *Danube School*, it was not in fact until the 18th century that water-colour became at all popular as a medium for landscapes, although a few isolated examples of 17th century "pioneers", like Van Dyck, should be mentioned. A drawing like plate 11, however, must have appealed more to the early 19th century taste for scenes stimulating to the imagination and its German title *Morgendämmerung* illustrates this aspect of its character.

Plate 12 *Virgin with a Multitude of Animals*. Probably 1503. Pen and water-colour. $12^5/_8 \times 9^9/_{16}$ in. (32.1 × 24.3 cm.). Vienna, Albertina.

The present drawing is exceptional on many counts, a scene of apparently unprecedented subject-matter, fully composed in water-colour, in which Dürer has used several of his early water-colours as preparatory drawings. To some critics it has suggested a recreation of the Garden of Eden but whatever the actual theme may be, it fully expresses Dürer's sympathy for animals, and his abilities as a draughts-man of plants and landscape.

Plate 13 *Virgin adoring the Infant Jesus*. Size colour on canvas. $37^3/_8 \times 41^1/_2$ in. (95 × 105.5 cm.). Dresden, Gemäldegalerie.

This, Dürer's first known religious painting, was made on commission for Frederick the Wise, Duke of Saxony, who visited Nuremberg in April 1496 and ordered a portrait from Dürer (now in Berlin) and two altarpieces for the Schlosskirche at Wittenberg which he had started to build in 1490. The second, "Ober St. Veit", altarpiece was painted largely by Dürer's workshop and is an altogether less revealing painting than the present one. This, the "Dresden altarpiece", now has two wings of SS. Anthony and Sebastian, which are on coarser canvas and may have been added in the plague year, 1502, although possibly not by Dürer himself. The theme of the Virgin adoring the Child is common in Flemish painting and the treatment here recalls Bouts perhaps more than any other Northern painter. However, by placing the Child on a ledge, Dürer shows knowledge of Italian compositions, associated with painters like Bellini, who sought to suggest in this way the added meaning that the scene was a prefiguration of the *Pietà*. The corpse-like character of the Child in Dürer's picture is particularly remarkable. With the cherubim, likewise Italian in origin, the chronologically later theme of the coronation of the Virgin is hinted at. The two topmost cherubs are, however, shown only in part, and this suggests that the picture has been considerably cut at the top.

Plate 14 *Hercules Killing the Stymphalian Birds.* Date, 1500 (renewed?). Size colour on canvas. $34^1/_4 \times 43^5/_{16}$ in. (87 × 110 cm.). Nuremberg, Germanisches National-Museum.

The theory that the present picture formed part of a decorative series known to have furnished a room in the castle of Frederick the Wise at Wittenberg and consisting of four pictures on the subject of Hercules is tempting to accept and would explain the extraordinary character of the painting. However, one study has survived for this picture and on the assumption that all four pictures were commissioned from Dürer, one might expect to find preparatory drawings for one or two of the other subjects. As with the Dresden Altarpiece, the cut-off figures along the upper margin suggest that the picture was originally higher. Although Dürer realised in engraving a number of classical subjects, both well-known and obscure, painting commissions gave him practically no opportunity to deal with such themes.

Plates 15 and 16 *Triptych, the Nativity with Saints George and Eustace. (The Paumgärtner Altarpiece).* Oil on wood. Centre panel $61 \times 49^5/_8$ in. (155 × 126 cm.), wings $60^1/_4 \times 24$ in. (153 × 61 cm.), each. Munich, Alte Pinakothek.

Painted for the Paumgärtner chapel of the Katherinen-kirche at Nuremberg. The traditional date is of 1498, when the picture may have been commissioned by the Paumgärtner family, but the centre panel is probably of 1502-4 and the wings slightly earlier (?) in date. Like the preceding picture, the general impression given by the central panel here is of a strong Flemish character and the figures of the shepherds, for example, have been compared with those in the work of Hugo van der Goes. The typically Northern motif of a wooden "lean-to" is, however, combined with an elaborate perspective construction generally found in Italian interpretations of the place of Christ's birth. Thoroughly typical of the Nor-

thern tradition again are the small scale figures of the donors and their children and an Annunciation painted of the backs of the wings of which only a part survives and that apparently executed in Dürer's workshop. The fronts of the wings, of Saints George and Eustace, are closer to Dürer's more personal experiments as revealed in his figure drawings of 1502-4, and the St George, underneath his suit of armour, is fairly close in pose to the engraved Adam (Fig. 3). The tradition that the two saints are portraits of Georg and Lucas Paumgärtner is highly probable for the heads seem, even for Dürer, to have too much individual character to be idealisations.

Plate 17 *Adoration of the Kings.* Monogram and date, 1504. Oil on wood. $38^9/_{16} \times 47^1/_4$ in. (98 × 112 cm.). Florence, Galleria degli Uffizi.

The present picture was probably ordered for the Schloss-kirche at Wittenberg but already in the early seventeenth century it was in the Imperial Kunstkammer at Vienna where it remained until 1792. At some time the group seems to have been augmented by the figure of St Joseph painted in probably behind the Virgin, where the surface of the panel now appears disturbed. Attempts have been made to connect it with another picture of Job and his wife and two musicians (one of whom is clearly a self-portrait) now divided into two panels (Frankfurt). This is the third of Dürer's major paintings of the period 1500-5; it was likewise at Wittenberg and may well have originally corresponded in size and shape with the present picture. The influence of Leonardo can be detected already in this picture. The king standing behind the Virgin is strikingly Leonardesque, while the figure of the kneeling king, the motif of the prancing horse in the background and certain architectural features, are probably distant echoes of Leonardo's unfinished *Adoration of the Magi* of about 1480 (Florence). The picture contains also one of the earliest examples of Dürer's monogram seen in perspective and pointing towards the main subject thus taking, as it were, a more active part in the scene and leading on to those later pictures where Dürer felt impelled to include his own undisguised portrait.

Plates 18 and 19 *Lot and his daughters fleeing from Sodom and Gomorrah. The Virgin in half length.* Oil on wood. $20^7/_8 \times 16^1/_8$ in. (53 × 41 cm.). Washington, National Gallery of Art, Samuel H. Kress Collection. The Madonna can be dated to about 1498-9 and the Lot, on the reverse, was probably executed shortly before this.

The history of the picture is known only as far back as 1932 when it was sold, bearing the significant attribution to Giovanni Bellini. Shortly afterwards it was recognised as a Dürer, with similarities to the *Self Portrait* (Pl. 20). One of the shields (Pl. 19, bottom left) was at the same time identified as that of the Heller family. It can be related to Bellini in only a very general way and is perhaps closer in some respects to Antonello da Messina and to other Venetian-inspired painters like Carlo Crivelli.

Plate 20 *Self Portrait*. Inscribed and dated 1498, with monogram. Oil on wood. 20$^1/_2$ × 16$^1/_8$ in. (52 × 41 cm.). Madrid, Museo del Prado.

This portrait has a strong claim to being the first independent self-portrait in the history of art. It was presented, together with a portrait of Dürer's father (probably the picture now in the National Gallery, London, referred to in the note to Pl. 1) by the city of Nuremberg to Charles I of England through the Earl of Arundel in 1636 and went to Spain not long afterwards. The present Royal Collection contains a portrait of an unknown man of 1506, which appears to be the only authentic painting by Dürer in this country (see note to Pl. 28).

Plate 21 *Self Portrait*. Monogram and date 1500 and inscription in Latin (all renewed). Oil on wood. 26$^3/_8$ × 19$^5/_{16}$ in. (67 × 49 cm.). Munich, Alte Pinakothek.

The third of Dürer's painted self-portraits; the inscriptions are later additions, although the date seems to be accurate, and the face is said to be repainted, conceivably by Dürer himself.

Plate 22 *Portrait of Elspeth Tucher*. Dated 1499. Oil on wood. 11 × 8$^{11}/_{16}$ in. (28 × 22 cm.). Inscribed: "Elspet Niclas Tuchern 26 Act". Kassel, Gemäldegalerie.

Three portraits by Dürer of members of the Tucher family are known: the pendant pictures of Hans and Felicitas, which were at Weimar but disappeared, apparently, just after the Second World War, and the present painting, which was presumably accompanied by a portrait of the husband of the sitter, Nicolas Tucher, whose name is given in the inscription and whose initials are the main feature of the clasp across the bodice of his wife. The three extant portraits correspond closely in size and character and must originally have made up a set of four. If Dürer intended to convey some personal comment through the pictures it may be relevant that the two female figures are seen against decidedly cloudy skies and the male figure has behind him a clear sky with a church in the landscape beneath. Apart from the two Weimar pictures, other major war-losses of Dürer's works include collections of drawings which were at Bremen and Dresden.

Plate 23 *Portrait of Oswolt Krell* (with shutters). Inscribed and dated 1499. Oil on wood. 18$^7/_8$ × 14$^{15}/_{16}$ in. (48 × 38 cm.), same dimensions for shutters. Munich, Alte Pinakothek.

The closest pictorial analogies to the present portrait are to be found in Bellini's late designs for the Madonna and Child theme, where a plain curtain together with a prospect of tall trees is a fairly common motif.

Plate 24 *Portrait of a Girl*. Monogram and date, 1505. Oil on wood. 13$^3/_4$ × 8$^1/_2$ in. (35 × 20.6 cm.). Vienna, Kunsthistorisches Museum.

This and the following portrait have been related to lost portraits by Bellini, known now only through drawings. The sitter's dress is apparently Milanese and a journey to Milan, where Dürer would have gained first-hand experience of Leonardo's school, has also been suggested.

Plate 25 *Portrait of a Young Woman*. Probably 1506-7. Oil on wood. 11$^1/_4$ × 8$^1/_4$ in. (28.5 × 21.5 cm.). False (?) monogram. Berlin-Dahlem, Staatliche Museen, Gemäldegalerie.

Although not dated, this portrait is clearly more Venetian in character than the last and must therefore have been painted at a later date. Some critics go so far as to suggest a date after Dürer's return to Nuremberg. The sitter was once believed to be Agnes Dürer because of the initials A D on her bodice but she bears no resemblance to Dürer's wife. Judging, however, by the Tucher portraits (Pl. 22) it was a German habit to display the husband's initials across the bodice, and the present sitter may well have been German even though her dress is unmistakably Italian.

Plate 26 *The Virgin with the Siskin*. Inscribed in Latin and dated 1506, with monogram. Oil on wood. 35$^{13}/_{16}$ × 29$^1/_2$ in. (91 × 75 cm.). Berlin-Dahlem, Staatliche Museen, Gemäldegalerie.

It has been demonstrated in the case of this picture that Dürer exerted an influence on Venetian art, a repayment as it were for his considerable debt to Venice. The figure of St John, itself a motif which Dürer had probably taken from Italian compositions, was used by Titian in an early picture, *The Madonna of the Cherries*, of the 1510s(?) (Vienna). This figure was originally an almost direct transcription of Dürer's St John, although it was later altered by Titian. Apart from the figure of St John, the composition is close in a general way to Bellini's half-length Madonna designs, although the landscape background includes passages reminiscent of the 1504 *Adoration of the Kings* (Pl. 17) and the super-abundant symbolism and activity is uncharacteristic of Bellini. Many of the symbols are clearly references to the death and passion of Christ. The siskin, the bird perched on Christ's arm, which gives its name to the picture, is apparently a finch and may, like the gold-finch which pecks thorns, refer to the crown of thorns, while Christ's death is probably implied by the lilies proffered by St John from which the Child seems shyly to recoil. The attitude of the Madonna is curious for she appears psychologically remote from the scene and Dürer may perhaps have intended to suggest the calm and untroubled character of Bellini's Madonnas.

Plates 27 and 28 *The Feast of the Rose-Garlands (Das Rosenkranzfest)*. Inscribed in Latin on a paper held by the artist and dated 1506, with monogram. Oil on wood.

$63^3/_4 \times 76^9/_{16}$ in. (162 × 194.5 cm.). Prague, National Gallery.

This, perhaps Dürer's most important single work, looks very different now from when it was first painted. Major losses, including nearly all the heads and much of the central part of the picture, were made up in the 19th century with little regard in some cases for recreating the original appearance of the work. In particular, the faces of the Virgin and Child are wholly uncharacteristic of Dürer and unlike early copies of the picture. It was carried off in the early 17th century from St Bartolomeo, the church of the German colony at Venice, for which it had been commissioned in 1506, to form part of the Royal collection at Prague. In his letters to Pirkheimer from Venice, Dürer speaks a good deal about the painting and the stir it caused when exhibited for the first time. Apparently, the Patriarch of Venice was impressed and Giovanni Bellini also. Dürer does not name any of the younger Venetian painters who may have seen and admired his work, but the Germans who commissioned it were slightly later to employ Giorgione and Titian to decorate the façade of their 'club', the Fondaco dei Tedeschi, with the frescoes which have now almost completely faded, but whose significance for the history of Venetian painting can still be discerned (1508). One connection between the two commissions is provided by the portrait in Dürer's altarpiece of an architect (extreme right and Pl. 30), probably Master Hieronymus (of Augsburg?) who was responsible for the rebuilding of the Fondaco after it had been burnt down in January 1505. Apart from the main figures, none of the other portraits has been satisfactorily identified, although Dürer made a separate portrait of one man (fourth from the left) which is the picture of 1506 now in the Royal collection.

Plates 29 and 30 *Study for the mantle of the Pope in "The Feast of the Rose-Garlands"*. False monogram and date, 1514. Water-colour. $16^{13}/_{16} \times 11^5/_{16}$ in. (42.7 × 28.8 cm.). Vienna, Albertina. *Study for the Architect in "The Feast of the Rose-Garlands"*. Monogram and date 1506. Brush, heightened with white, on blue Venetian paper. $15^3/_{16} \times 10^3/_8$ in. (38.6 × 26.3 cm.). Berlin-Dahlem, Staatliche Museen, Kupferstichkabinett.

Two of about 19 surviving studies for the Rosenkranzfest. The architect is probably identifiable with Master Hieronymus (of Augsburg?; see note to Pl. 27 above). Many of the drawings are for the heads of cherubs which Dürer did not finally use for the finished picture but kept and introduced into the Heller altarpiece. They thus provide a connection between what are probably Dürer's two most ambitious paintings and suggest that Dürer himself saw some parallel between the two.

Plate 31 *Christ among the Doctors*. Monogram and date, 1506. Oil on wood. $25^5/_8 \times 31^1/_2$ in. (65 × 80 cm.).

Inscribed: "Opus quinque dierum". Lugano, Thyssen Collection.

It is probably this picture to which Dürer refers as "the like of which I have never painted before" in a letter sent to Pirkheimer from Venice and he is certainly right in this judgment. He may have been inspired by certain compositions by Mantegna or Bellini, for example, designed exclusively in terms of half-length figures and perhaps by a similar composition of the same subject which Leonardo may have designed. Leonardo was asked in 1504 by Isabella d'Este for a picture of the single figure of Christ disputing and the existence of a picture of *Christ amongst the Doctors* by his pupil, Luini (National Gallery, London), suggests that Leonardo had got some way with the design of a fully elaborated version of this subject. Although Luini's picture is quite unlike Dürer's in character, the design is similar and certain motifs, like the head-dress of the man in the right foreground in each picture, are remarkably similar. In both, the figure nearest to Christ on the right is rather more of a caricature than the other figures and the one in Luini's picture could almost have been copied directly from Leonardo's drawings. One unusual feature of Dürer's picture is the three-pointed aureole of Christ; for it is a translation into terms of paint of a type of aureole found elsewhere only in his graphic representations of Christ (Fig. 10).

Plate 32 *Study for a hand in "Christ among the Doctors"*. Brush, heightened with white, on blue Venetian paper. $7^1/_2 \times 9^7/_8$ in. (19 × 25.1 cm.). Vienna, Albertina.

One of four surviving drawings for the *Christ among the Doctors*. Two others are likewise studies of hands and one, originally joined to a sheet with a study for the angel in the Rosenkranzfest, is for the head of Christ.

Plate 33 *Adam and Eve*. Inscribed in Latin and dated 1507, with monogram. Oil on wood. $82^9/_{16} \times 31^7/_8$ in. and $32^{13}/_{16}$ in. respectively (209 × 81 and 83 cm.). Madrid, Museo del Prado.

Drawings for the present picture were begun by Dürer in Venice (Fig. 12) and they suggest that he may originally have intended the subject as an engraving or woodcut for the figures are drawn on both sides of the paper with one side silhouetted to show how the figure would look in reverse. They are unlike Dürer's other preparatory drawings for paintings but similar, for example, to those for the engraving of Adam and Eve of 1504 or to illustrations of proportions. In all these drawings the figures are also articulated by means of construction lines. As paintings the present panels are rather curious for they are similar in character and size to works like the wings of the Paumgärtner Altarpiece (Pl. 15) and the *Four Saints* (Pl. 50) which serve, or were intended originally to serve, a particular function as shutters.

Plate 34 *Martyrdom of the Ten Thousand Christians*. Inscribed on a paper held by the artist, dated 1508, with monogram. Oil on wood, transferred to canvas. 39 × 22⁷/₁₆ in. (99 × 57 cm.). Vienna, Kunsthistorisches Museum.

Dürer refers to the present picture commissioned by Frederick of Saxony in two of his letters to Jacob Heller, describing perhaps with some exaggeration the progress of the work which was finished during the spring of 1508. A preparatory drawing shows that the picture was originally intended to be an oblong composition and at this stage Dürer appears as a lone figure walking near the foreground. The final picture is closer to the woodcut of 1508 but with the group of Bishop Archatius and a torturer drilling out his eyes omitted, and the theme of the three crosses introduced. Dürer has also taken a companion with him into the picture, who was been identified as the humanist Conrad Celtes.

Plate 35 *Assumption and Coronation of the Virgin* (Copy of the centre panel of *The Heller Altarpiece*). Oil on wood. 72⁷/₈ × 53⁵/₁₆ in. (185 × 135.4 cm.). Frankfurt-am-Main, Historisches Museum.

This copy of Dürer's central panel (1509) of the triptych commissioned by Jacob Heller for the St Thomas altar in the Dominican church at Frankfurt was executed by Jobst Harrich before the sale of the original to Maximilian of Bavaria in 1614. The original was subsequently burnt in 1729 in Munich. The negotiations between Dürer and Jacob Heller for the picture are fully documented in the series of 8 letters, from which representative passages are quoted in the section dealing with Dürer's writings. Much of the correspondence concerns money, and Dürer was able eventually to raise the price from 130 to 200 florins. About 20 surviving drawings (not including the ones of cherub heads drawn originally for the Rosenkranzfest) show also how carefully he planned the work and the letters with his patron range over several years. Dürer seems therefore to have attached more than usual significance to the picture, and the nature of his achievement can still be felt even in the present copy. The shutters of the altarpiece still survive (Frankfurt) but as Dürer admitted in his letters they are workshop products, and seem poor in quality. Far more interesting are the panels by Grünewald, which are generally believed to have acted as fixed wings for the altarpiece. The upper parts of these wings, have been identified as the pictures of Saints Lawrence and Cyriacus, which are now in Frankfurt and the lower parts are probably the panels of St Elizabeth of Thuringia and an unknown female martyr at Donaueschingen. These figures are very different in character from Dürer's saints, more irrationally expressive and altogether softer in modelling. The fixed wings and the central panel are both, however, a tribute to the discerning taste of Jacob Heller.

Plates 36 and 37 *The Adoration of the Trinity*. Inscribed and dated 1511, with monogram. Oil on wood. 53¹/₈ × 48⁵/₈

in. (135 × 123.4 cm.). Vienna, Kunsthistorisches Museum. Painted for Matthaeus Landauer for the Chapel dedicated to All Saints in the Zwölfbrüderhaus, Nuremberg. *Composition study for "The Adoration of the Trinity"*. Monogram and date, 1508. Pen and water-colour. 15³/₈ × 10³/₈ in. (39.1 × 26.3 cm.). Chantilly, Musée Condé.

The drawing shows how Dürer had originally conceived the composition on simpler lines apparently excluding the laymen from the bottom tier, which is inhabited by ecclesiastics and Old Testament figures. In the finished picture, the latter (Moses, for example, clearly recognisable with the tablets of the Law) were promoted to the second tier and figures like Matthaeus Landauer, on the right, and the emperor (left), have taken their places. Originally the frame was also simpler with plain columns flanking a square picture. The semi-circular scene of Judgment was probably based on the Old Testament portals of Gothic Cathedrals like the one of St Lorenz at Nuremberg and it is a capital example of Dürer's ability to use a familiar motif in an alien and fundamentally Italian context. The final picture is certainly Dürer's most crowded pictorial composition, the closest analogies being with the Apocalypse woodcut series (Fig. 3), but its organisation is managed with enormous skill. The four main figures in the bottom row are complementary in pose and linked by means of colour: from left to right, a cardinal (red) facing outwards, the pope (gold) looking inwards, and emperor (gold) looking out and a second emperor (red) looking in. In the very centre is a figure in blue, the colour of the river beneath and the robes of God the Father above. Red and gold play a smaller part in the upper part of the picture where more ethereal greens and blues predominate The chief female martyr in blue, faces across to the principal male saint in green and both colours are united with small areas of gold and red in the figure of God the Father. Although the picture is conceived more in terms of groups than of single figures, it is organised with the same rational clarity as the Heller altarpiece.

Plate 38 *The Virgin with the Pear*. Monogram and date, 1512. Oil on wood. 19¹/₄ × 14⁹/₁₆ in. (49 × 37 cm.). Vienna, Kunsthistorisches Museum.

With the tremendous revival of interest in Dürer in the seventeenth century, when churches and private collections, were subject to Imperial depredations, pictures like the present one which may have belonged to Dürer's friend, Willibald Pirkheimer and was perhaps in the collection of Rudolph II, became much sought after. A picture of the Virgin in prayer by Sassoferrato (1609-1685) in Sta. Maria della Salute in Venice seems to have been based on this particular painting by Dürer.

Plate 39 *The Virgin in Prayer*. Monogram and date, 1518. Oil on wood. 20⁷/₈ × 16¹⁵/₁₆ in. (53 × 43 cm.). Berlin-Dahlem, Staatliche Museen, Gemäldegalerie.

Painting played only a small part in Dürer's work in the late 1510s and the harsh lighting, bright colours and fussy drapery in this picture exemplify the apparently retrogressive character of his handling of paint. The subject of the picture is presumably the Virgin Annunciate.

Plate 40 *Portrait of Michael Wolgemut.* Inscriptions, monogram and date 1516. Oil on wood. 11⁷/₁₆ × 10⁵/₈ in. (29 × 27 cm.). Nuremberg, Germanisches Museum.

The inscriptions on the present picture refer to Wolgemut's role as Dürer's mentor, and to his death in 1519, and it was probably for Dürer's own satisfaction that the portrait was executed. (See the note to Pl. 1.)

Plate 41 *Portrait of Maximilian I.* Inscribed, with monogram and date, 1519. Oil on wood. 28⁷/₈ × 20¹/₁₆ in. (73 × 61.5 cm.). Vienna, Kunsthistorisches Museum.

Dürer painted a second version of this portrait but on canvas (Nuremberg) and this is conceivably the picture which he offered unacceptably to the regent of the Netherlands in 1520 (see his diary). In both pictures the emperor carries a pomegranate (as a symbol of immortality) but this he holds with both hands in the Nuremberg version and there exists a preparatory drawing (Albertina) for this motif. In the present picture one hand rests on an unseen ledge in the bottom right hand corner. This characteristically Flemish device, often used by Dürer in bust-length portraits (Pl. 43) is combined somewhat unnaturally with a formalised half-length. Dürer, it seems, felt impelled to redraw the hands and thus to change the pose of the emperor for what must have been the later (canvas) version of the picture.

Plate 42 One of the forty-five marginal illustrations in the *Prayer Book of Maximilian I.* Dated 1515. Pen (red, violet or green ink) on vellum. Each 10¹³/₁₆ × 7¹/₂ in. (27.5 × 19 cm.). Munich, Staatsbibliothek. *Two musicians and hermit; lion and a dragonfly* (green). (dd) fol. 38 verso; with monogram. This plate is reproduced from the facsimile edition published by Georg Franz.

The prayer book was compiled by Maximilian and intended for members of his order of St George, instigated in connection with a possible new Crusade. In 1515 Dürer had completed ten quires of the book, it was then passed on to other German painters. Lucas Cranach the Elder amongst them; the manuscript is now divided between Munich and Besançon. The function of the book as an imitation Gothic Manuscript, is, of course, thoroughly in character with Maximilian's projects of chivalry, and Dürer's illustrations combine classical scrolls and motifs in a fine disarray characteristic of the Late Gothic style and comparable with his triumphal arch also designed for Maximilian (see p. 22). The present illustration has been connected with a phrase in the accompanying text and probably shows man as the master of all creatures.

Plate 43 *Portrait of an Unknown Man.* Dated 1524 (?). Oil on wood. 19¹¹/₁₆ × 14³/₁₆ in. (50 × 36 cm.). Madrid, Museo del Prado.

The date on the present portrait was originally read as 1521 and the picture identified with a lost portrait of Jobst Plankfelt, Dürer's host in Antwerp during his visit to the Netherlands. The portrait shows, however, a later and probably grander sitter. It is, however, thoroughly Netherlandish in character, and close in its composition to a portrait of Bernhard von Resten (Dresden) which Dürer did in fact paint on his journey. For all its simplicity the picture is nevertheless designed with enormous care, in particular the line of disturbed fur running across the sitter's left lapel contributes subtly to the stability of the design.

Plate 44 *Portrait of Hieronymus Holzschuher.* Inscribed and dated 1526, with monogram. Oil on wood. 18⁷/₈ × 14³/₁₆ in. (48 × 36 cm.). Berlin-Dahlem, Staatliche Museen, Gemäldegalerie.

Dürer here returned to a more concentrated form of portrait which he had used at least since 1500 (*Anonymous Male Portrait*, Munich). The design of the head and shoulders is closely related to the preceding portrait although the sitter here confronts the spectator. The companion portrait of Jacob Muffel, who was, like Holzschuher, a senator of Nuremberg, is close in character although the sitter wears a hat and looks directly to the left. Both have inscriptions in Roman letters in the upper right corners, and in this respect they resemble Dürer's late engraved and drawn portraits (Pl. 46).

Plate 45 *Portrait of Johannes Kleberger.* Inscribed, with monogram and date, 1526. Oil on wood. 14⁹/₁₆ × 14⁹/₁₆ in. (37 × 37 cm.). Vienna, Kunsthistorisches Museum.

This, the most extraordinary of Dürer's painted portraits is of an equally extraordinary sitter. Son of a poor expatriate of Nuremberg who returned to his home-town a wealthy man; in 1528 he married Felicitas the daughter of Dürer's friend Willibald Pirkheimer, and left again shortly afterwards for Lyons where he gave his fortune away to charity and died.

Plate 46 *Portrait of Ulrich Starck.* Monogram and date 1526. Chalk. 16¹/₈ × 11⁵/₈ in. (41 × 29.6 cm.). London, British Museum.

One of the last and most splendid of the chalk presentation portraits which were executed by Dürer from the time of his journey to the Netherlands onwards.

Plate 47 *The Annunciation.* Monogram and date, 1526. Pen and water-colour. 11⁵/₁₆ × 8⁵/₁₆ in. (28.8 × 21.1 cm.). Chantilly, Musée Condé.

The predominantly rectilinear pen strokes and the strikingly neat organisation of the present drawing are characteristic of Dürer's late style. In showing the angel actually handing a letter to the Virgin, Dürer adopts a rare and apparently old-fashioned iconographical type, as he does also in the following drawing (Pl. 48) where Christ is shown with his feet nailed separately to the cross.

Plate 48 *Christ on the Cross*. With date, 1523, and half the monogram. Metalpoint, heightened with white, on green grounded paper. 16⁷/₈ × 11¹³/₁₆ in. (41.3 × 30 cm.). Paris, Musée du Louvre.

A study for the engraving *The Great Crucifixion*. One of about 13 drawings executed around 1523 for an engraving of the crucifixion. Only about a sixth of the plate was finished, the rest of the composition being indicated in outline only and it therefore provides valuable evidence about Dürer's method of engraving. The composition seems to have been based on a pen drawing of 1521 showing only Christ, the Virgin and St John (Vienna) which was then considerably elaborated in a series of drawings in chalk or, like the present example, in metalpoint on green prepared paper. The latter technique was a new one and therefore characteristic of Dürer's urge for experiment in his later years, while the idea of making such thorough studies for an engraving is itself a new departure for Dürer. It is curious that he never completed a work prepared so scrupulously, but it would have lacked the simplicity characteristic of Dürer's other late works and the artist may therefore have felt little sympathy with the final product.

Plate 49 *The Virgin with the Pear*. Monogram and date 1526. Oil on wood. 16¹⁵/₁₆ × 12⁵/₈ in. (43 × 32 cm.). Florence, Galleria degli Uffizi.

Though the present picture has been treated by some critics with suspicion, the signature and condition in particular, it illustrates nevertheless on a small scale the characteristics of Dürer's latest style. The frontality and clear organisation forming a contrast with a similar work of 1512 (Pl. 38). The facial types of the figures, less outwardly expressive, and closer in character to geometrical solids, are the embodiment in paint of the round-faced child and sharp-featured Madonna in his contemporary drawings (Fig. 14).

Plate 50 *Saints John the Evangelist and Peter, Mark and Paul* (called "*The Four Apostles*"). With inscriptions, monogram and date, 1526. Oil on wood. 80⁹/₁₆ × 29¹/₈ in. (204 × 74 cm.) each. Munich. Alte Pinakothek.

The development of these panels has been only summarily described in the text though it is knowledge essential for understanding the character of the pictures. It appears that the St Paul (the principal figure of the right hand panel) was painted originally about 1523 as a figure of St Philip, corresponding, as alterations in the picture show, with an engraving of St Philip finished in that year but not finally issued until 1526 and then with a corrected date. Dürer probably intended this early picture to serve as the right hand wing, with St Philip's companion saint, James the Lesser, represented on the opposite wing, as the shutters of his "sacra conversazione" (Fig. 14). This commission was presumably withdrawn and in 1525 Dürer made a preparatory drawing for St John the Evangelist the main figure on the left hand wing. The St Philip was changed into a representation of St Paul and the figures of Sts Peter and Mark were added to the background of the wings. In 1526 Dürer presented the wings to the Town Council of Nuremberg and finally issued the print of St Philip. This theory, which can be found set out in greater detail in Panofsky's book on Dürer, explains many of the peculiarities of the finished pictures. Why in the first place it should have been painted on two panels. Also St Paul is harder in style than the other figures which suggests an earlier date for his execution. He takes up almost the whole of the right hand panel, and presumably was originally self-sufficient. The interpretation of the symbolism of the picture is not purely speculative, for Johann Neudörffer, who worked on the lettering of the quotations on the bottom of the panels, claimed that Dürer intended the figures to illustrate the four temperaments, and this is therefore a definite starting-point for unravelling the hidden meaning of the work.

I

2

4

5

8

9

weier Haus

10

II

13

14

15

17

19

23

24

25

27

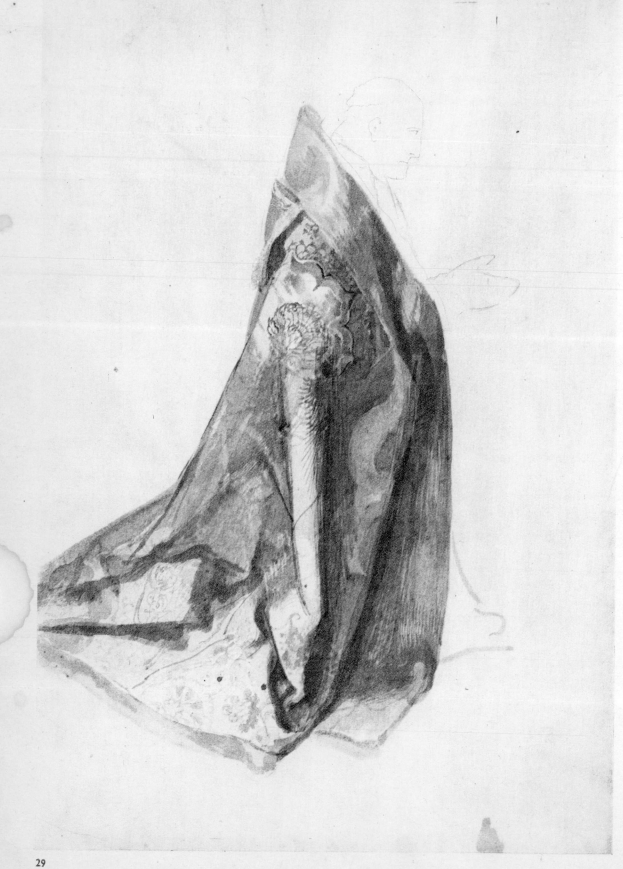

29

31

32

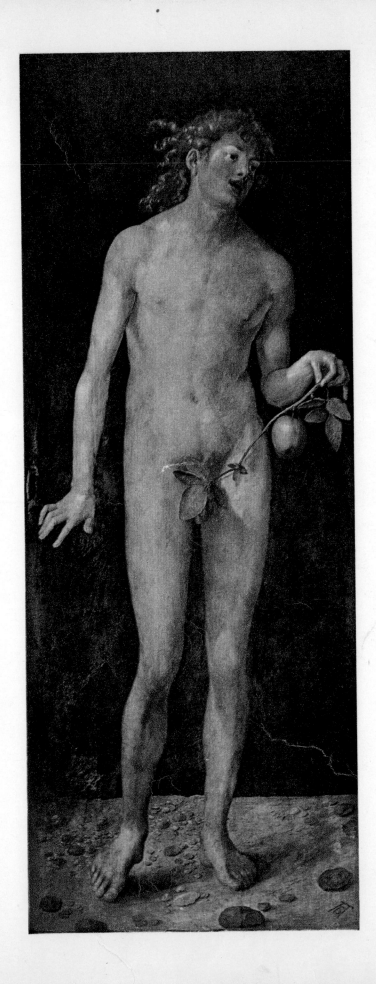

POTENTISSIMVS · MAXIMVS · ET · INVICTISSIMVS · CÆSAR · MAXIMILIANVS
QVI · CVNCTOS · SVI · TEMPORIS · REGES · ET · PRINCIPES · IVSTICIA · PRVDENCIA
MAGNANIMILITATE · LIBERALITATE · PRÆCIPVE · VERO · BELLICA · LAVDE · ET
ANIMI · FORTITVDINE · SVPERAVIT · NATVS · EST · ANNO · SALVTIS · HVMANÆ
M · CCCC · LIX · DIE · MARCII · IX · VIXIT · ANNOS · LIX · MENSES · IX · DIES · XXV
DECESSIT · VERO · ANNO · M · D · XIX · MENSIS · IANVARII · DIE · XII · QVEM · DEVS
OPT · MAX · IN · NVMERVM · VIVENCIVM · REFERRE · VELIT ·

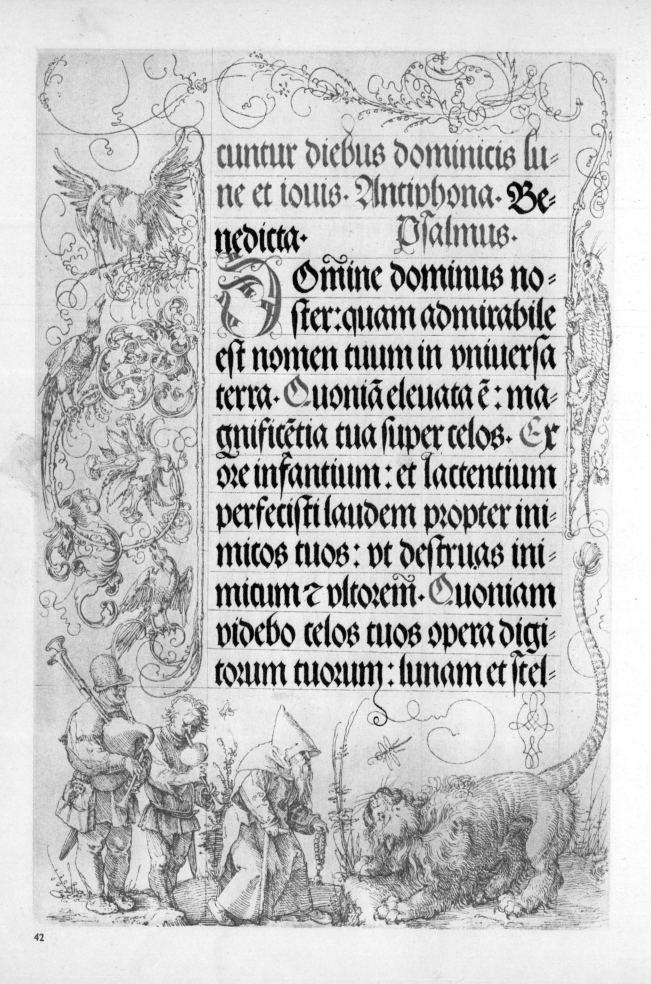

cuntur diebus dominicis lu=
ne et iouis. Antiphona. Be=
nedicta. Psalmus.

Omine dominus no=
ster:quam admirabile
est nomen tuum in vniuersa
terra. Quoniã eleuata ẽ: ma=
gnificẽtia tua super celos. Ex
ore infantium: et lactentium
perfecisti laudem propter ini=
micos tuos: vt destruas ini
micum ᷓ vltorem. Quoniam
videbo celos tuos opera digi=
torum tuorum: lunam et stel

44

1529

46

1523

50